THE DIAR SOUTHPOR**Paul Bagshaw**

Artworks

2001

First published in 2001
by Artworks
46 Lyndhurst Road, Southport PR8 4JT.
www.artworks-pictures.co.uk

Printed by Mitchell & Wright Printers Limited,
Banastre Road, Southport PR8 5AL.
All rights reserved

ISBN 0 9541592 0 9

Acknowledgements:
To Dom Wulstan Probert OSB,
Eric Appleton, R. Marshall, Alan Martin,
Stan and Carol Hutchinson, Bamforth & Co,
Rimmer Watson & Co, Southport Corporation and
Andrew Farthing of Southport Reference Library
for kindly providing photographic material,
to Philip and Brenda McFadyen and to
Ronald Johns who put up with having
the book read to them in Provence, and
to Peter Ravenscroft and John Rostron
for their patience in proof-reading.

THE DIARY OF A SOUTHPORT BOY

Paul Bagshaw

CONTENTS

PART ONE
IN THE BEGINNING
1937-46

PART TWO
PREP SCHOOL DAYS
1946-49

IN THE BEGINNING
1937-46

PROMS AND PRAMS
THE DAY I MET ADOLF HITLER
POETIC JUSTICE
ANOTHER LOSS
THE BOY WHO COMMITTED ADULTERY
FRIENDS AND NEIGHBOURS
THE DEMISE OF UNCLE JACK
MUSIC AND THEATRES
INTO THE BIG SCHOOL

1937193719371937193719371937193719371937

PROMS AND PRAMS

Although it may seem presumptuous of me to claim that my birth
in Southport on December 1st 1937 was an event of some importance, it was
nevertheless true. This was because my mother was then thirty-nine and
had miscarried twelve months previously, and so I was quite possibly her
very last opportunity to bear a child safely. She was my father's second
wife, his first having died young, leaving Rita, aged five, and Denis,
aged three, motherless. My parents first met on Bournemouth promenade
during a late summer holiday, and my father proposed marriage to her
three days later. Quite sensibly, she rejected the suggestion on the basis
that they could not possibly know each other well enough to consider such
a step, but he was not to be put off. After the holiday, he wrote to her
three times a day - when the post was more frequent than at present - and
also sent her bouquets of flowers on a daily basis. His perseverance paid
off and, just three months after first meeting in 1926, they were married.

My father, Gilbert Bagshaw, was born in Cleckheaton, Yorkshire,
in 1893. He was educated at Heckmondwike School and, later, at Chester
College where he trained as a teacher. The story of his own father
remains something of a mystery, but he did have a brother Jack, who did
not marry and whose own life deserves a book all to itself. Gilbert served
in the armed forces as a musician in the First World War, and his posting
to India exposed him to yellow fever, which most probably shortened his
life by several years. He taught in Bournemouth and, after marrying for
the second time, later in Morecambe before his appointment to a teaching
post in Southport at Farnborough Road School, which I later attended as
a pupil in the early 1940s.

Lilian Hales, my mother, was brought up in Warrington. She was born in June 1898, with an elder brother, Louis, and two sisters, Monica and Mildred. One of her great sadnesses as a young woman were the deaths in the First World War of so many boys she had known socially at dances and parties, and this may well have accounted for her remaining single until the age of twenty-eight when she met Gilbert. It was a love match, and they had a great deal in common, not least a sense of humour, which they would need in order to face some of the difficulties that lay ahead. Amongst their shared interests were literature, poetry, drama and music, as well as the joy of giving and attending parties, and they were also quite accomplished bridge players.

When I was born the family lived at 46 Lyndhurst Road, Birkdale, in a three-bedroomed semi-detached house dating from 1928. It was smaller than the detached houses they had occupied in Bournemouth and Morecambe - they had a strong attraction to the seaside - and was considered as a temporary rented stopping point until they found somewhere larger. My father had very much wanted to buy 24 Lyndhurst Road, which was then on the market and which later became the Bullen School of Dance, but my mother objected on the grounds that it would cost a fortune to carpet, having a large studio incorporated into the house. When I was older and was told of this, I was most disappointed because, just like my father, I was tempted to rate exciting ideas a long way ahead of practical considerations, an expensive trait that I still display.

My baptism was somewhat controversial, although I remained unaware of this until much later. Our Parish Priest, Father F, was something of a snob and very much a Catholic of the old school. He did nothing to conceal his disapproval of my mother's marriage to an agnostic, and had expressed this view to her on a number of occasions, although it should be said that his curate did not share his opinion. Just before the ceremony began he was in an impatient mood, clearly displaying no appetite for the event and anxious to get it over as soon as possible. Then, he caught sight of my Godfather at the other end of the church. "Is that Dick Kendall?" he asked enthusiastically. Dick was a prominent Catholic layman in Preston, and he and his wife Hilda were close friends of our family. Father F then moved enthusiastically towards Dick and shook him by the hand. His entire manner changed, and he proceeded to conduct my baptism with a warmth hitherto unrevealed, to the disgust of my mother. Thus, oblivious of the intrigue surrounding this ceremony, I was baptised a Roman Catholic in the Parish of Our Lady of Lourdes, Birkdale, where I worship still.

One of the characteristics of looking back to an early period in life is the difficulty of distinguishing between what we actually remember of

The author, his mother and the pram

an event, and what we recall being told. The writer Compton Mackenzie claimed to remember being in his mother's womb. At the risk of appearing less perceptive, I must confess that my recollections do not reach back as far as that, yet I do vividly recall being not much more than a year old and travelling in an Osnath pram. The reason it remains in my memory was because of an incident that took place outside Heywood's Chip Shop at the top of our road. Whilst my mother was in the shop, I discovered that the wing-nuts attaching the hood to my pram were unscrewable. Simply to occupy myself during a rather uneventful period of waiting, I decided to see how many nuts could be removed before my mother returned. The answer was all of them. Nevertheless, the hood somehow remained in position until my mother started to push the pram. Passers-by were more amused than she was at the resulting collapse. Although the outcome was not pre-meditated - after all, I was still quite young - the experience gave me an appetite for future research, and taught me the gratification to be gained by making others laugh.

A second experience involving the same pram occurred some months later, although it was an episode about which I was told, rather than one I personally recalled. My father's great passion was the collecting of books, most particularly first editions. Consequently, he spent many contented hours in Broadhurst's Book Shop in Market Street, a book collector's mecca to this day. Because we had no car, he would sometimes push me in the pram into town, parking me outside the shop whilst he searched for interesting volumes. It is interesting to note that, in those days, children left in this way were not considered to be at risk. About three hours later he returned home and entered the house with a cheery, "Hello, dearest", and looking forward to his lunch. "Where's the baby?" asked my mother. "Oh, my God!" he cried, rushing out of the house and down the road to the bus stop. I was found, still outside the shop in my pram, singing, laughing, telling passers-by that I was 'eighteen months', and generally enjoying myself. My mother was greatly relieved at my return although, I rather hope, somewhat hurt that nobody considered me sufficiently attractive to abduct.

193919391939193919391939193919391939

THE DAY I MET ADOLF HITLER

As I approached the age of two I graduated from the large pram to a push-chair. This was much better, for it meant that I could travel on a bus with my mother, whilst the folded push-chair was stored under the stairs. Bus travel was a great adventure, for there were dozens of people to stare at and to talk to. I said hello to everyone who got on the bus and, although some of them did not say hello back, I was not discouraged. I was also most interested in the bus conductors and, in particular, their ticket machines. In those days they carried a block of wood with a row of spring clips to hold the sets of tickets of different colours and values, and a bright silver ticket punch held in place by a diagonal leather shoulder strap. To a child of my age, the witnessing of the ritual punching of tickets was quite magical, and my longing to be a bus conductor outweighed my wish to be a driver by some distance. In addition, there was the sheer delight of ringing the bell, and when I got home from these journeys, I would stand in the cupboard under the stairs acting out the role of the bus conductor for all I was worth, making the sound of the ringing of the bell as I said 'Hold tight, please', and asking people to move further down the bus to make room for others.

As my bus journeys became more frequent, I got to know particular conductors quite well. There was one who looked very like my brother, Denis, and another with a very long face who resembled Douglas Cardew Robinson, a long-forgotten comedy actor who played 'Cardew the Cad' in the thirties, forties and fifties. A third conductor was very short-sighted, for he wore jam-jar glasses that distorted the size of his eyes and made him look like something from outer space. However, by far the most distinguished of all the bus conductors was a man who wore his Southport Corporation peaked cap in the style of the Waffen SS. The crown curved upward in Nazi style and, looking back, I can only assume that he must have customised it to create this striking effect. Furthermore, he wore rimless spectacles identical to those of Heinrich Himmler, as well as a carefully-trimmed light brown moustache. He had a permanently sinister smile on his face, which added to his disturbing yet appealing countenance. The diagonal belt that held the ticket punch gave him a military look, and all he needed was a lüger in a holster and a Nazi armband to complete the illusion. However, this was far from being the only Third Reich image on the number 14 bus route at that time.

One day a man with a black toothbrush moustache and straight dark hair brushed over his forehead got onto the bus at Birkdale Station and sat opposite me on the side seats at the back of the downstairs saloon. I recognised him immediately. "Look, Mummy! There's Hitler!" I shouted at the top of my voice, pleased at my rapid and accurate exposing of this infamous character. The bus fell into a shocked silence, for I suppose the incident appeared less amusing during the war that it would be today. For weeks after that historic encounter I embarrassed my mother and countless innocent men of the district by the identifying, naming and shaming of Göring, Himmler, Goebbels, Mussolini, Churchill and others on the 14 route, as well as in Irwin's Grocers, Lang's Butchers, Seymour Meads, Sawyer's Greengrocers, Pickering's Chemists and Webster's Bread Shop. I must say that I was surprised at how much more quickly than everyone else I spotted these well-known personalities. I was from a household where there was quite a lot of discussion about the war and its politics, and I also saw frequently, even at that age, photographs and cartoons of the main players. Like many young children, I picked up and absorbed far more details of adult conversations and of radio broadcasts than my parents realised. As I recall, a very few of those exposed to my unmasking tactics saw the funny side of the situation, and one or two walked out of shops after I made my loud announcements, much to my mother's discomfort. At the time, all of this simply confirmed to me the accuracy of my perceptions.

19401940194019401940194019401940194019401940

POETIC JUSTICE

Why I include this section in the book I am not quite sure, for it contains verses from my mother about her 'little treasure'. The poem that follows was one of over twenty she wrote about me from birth up to the age of four.

Now I'm Three
Now I'm three I really must
Eat up every little crust.
Never leave upon my plate
Anything I could have ate.
Put my socks on by myself
And reach the very highest shelf.
I'm doing this because, you see,
A boy is grown up when he's three.

My mother's writing took many forms. Seven years previously, a letter she wrote to the News Chronicle was published in the book 'Vital Sayings of the Year 1933':

"Teachers' cuts are to remain, while increased expenditure for the Navy and Air Force is to be considered by the Treasury. In other words, money for creative purposes cannot be spared, but money to help destroy humanity and all that it has achieved will be handed over ungrudgingly!"

Her principal flair was found in the humorous letters she wrote to her family from time to time. One told of her sad death; a subsequent one of her funeral. However, a very real sadness prompted her to write a poem in 1942, marking the death of Rita, my step-sister, at the age of twenty-one, an event which left my father quite desolate.

When poetry is so many words
And music just as meaningless.
When baby fingers on my cheek
Receive no answ'ring soft caress.

x

When seagulls swooping home to shore
Become as planes from battle skies.
Then, only then, shall I forget
The smile that ever lit your eyes.

194219421942194219421942194219421942

ANOTHER LOSS

1942 was the year that Denis, my step-brother, joined the RAF, his sister Rita having joined the WAAF in the previous year. My father, who had served in the 1914-18 war, was considered too old to enter active service, but he was appointed fire warden for Lyndhurst Road, an important post if incendiary bombs were to fall in our area. The only bomb that landed in Birkdale, as far as I know, was on part of Farnborough Road School where my father taught and where I became a pupil. There was a story that the sandhills, stretching from Formby to Southport, were set on fire to act as a decoy in order to deceive German bombers into mistaking the area for Liverpool. I do not know how true the story is, but it seems to be supported by the number of bomb craters that were later found in this vicinity. There was also a fear, thankfully unrealised, that Hitler might be planning to invade this country from Ireland, because the beach that stretched from Southport to Formby Point would have made a perfect location for an amphibious landing.

Mr father had already suffered one major loss with the death of his first wife, the mother of Rita and Denis. To lose his only daughter, aged just twenty-one, wounded him deeply, and it is probable that he never really got over this misfortune. I was just four, so the event did not touch me in quite the same way as the others in the family. Nevertheless, I regretted that the laughing, energetic, red-haired young woman who had made such a fuss of me was no longer there. Above all, I remember seeing my father cry for the very first time, and that moved me

The author in his pedal car, with Denis, Rita and parents
12

much more strongly than the cause of his grieving. It brought home to me, doubtless in a sub-conscious way, that grown-ups can feel some of the same emotions that I had experienced and that they, too, were vulnerable.

Rita's death cast a shadow over our home for quite some time and, every so often, something would happen to bring back memories of the event. The most poignant of all was when Stuart, Rita's boyfriend and someone to whom she might well have become engaged, returned from his Army posting abroad and called, carrying a large bunch of flowers, at our house to see her, a year after her death. The grown-ups took Stuart into the front room to break the news to him, whilst I played in the garden. I can still recall his serious and resigned expression as he left the house. We did not see him again.

Rita had joined the Women's Auxiliary Air force at the age of twenty in 1941 and, in 1946, a medal inscribed with her name, attached to a distinctive blue, orange, silver and black ribbon and bearing the head of King George VI, was delivered by the postman one morning in a small cardboard box. Although its arrival inevitably reopened my father's grieving, he was immensely proud that she had been recognised in this way. Very much later, in the mid-1990s, the name of Rita Bagshaw was added to those on the Roll of Honour displayed on the Southport Monument in Lord Street.

THE BOY WHO COMMITTED ADULTERY

I looked forward to starting school and I was very proud of my new maroon and gold uniform. My optimism was drawn from the positive messages from my parents for weeks in advance and, inevitably, the knowledge that my father was a teacher there. Farnborough Road School was, and still is, a large school with a fine reputation. On the first day I was alarmed at the sight of a boy in a balaclava helmet, an item of headgear I had not previously encountered. Was this the bogey man I had heard about and who hid in air-raid shelters? At first we played a lot and the most popular toys were the two large wooden double-deck buses, which reduced children to tears if they thought that someone else had taken their turn to ride on them. In the morning we drank small bottles of milk, giving us all white moustaches, and each afternoon we had a half-hour sleep on our little bunk beds. We enjoyed painting, for which we were all issued with smocks to protect our clothes. We dipped long-handled brushes into watery powder paint in a range of Ostwald colours, in order to produce horrifying portraits of our parents. The other fun activity was music, for which we had a choice of castanets, tambourines and triangles. We stood in pairs in front of manuscript charts with large coloured notes, designed so that we should know when our turn to play came round. Since none of us could grasp the system quickly enough to play in time, the process failed completely, but I think we enjoyed it nevertheless. Every so often we would be told to put on our tiny gas masks as part of wartime drill, and I can still remember the distinctive smell of the filtered air we had to breathe. In no time at all, our gas masks would steam up, producing a roomful of sweaty and hyperactive infants running blindly into furniture and into each other.

I have forgotten the names of some of my teachers at that early stage, but I do remember well Miss Williams who was plump and wore pearls over a grey jumper, and also Miss Forshaw, with long hair and protruding teeth, who was jolly and kind to us all. The top infants class was taught by Miss Fazakerley who had a large oval of frizzy dark brown hair. She had a multi-coloured collection of wooden pointers, rather like conductors' batons, and I so much wanted one of these that I tried making one for myself at home, without much success. Another strong memory from her room was the range of appetising smells like newly-sharpened pencils and lavender floor polish. However, it was in Miss Fazakerley's class that I first succumbed to crime. Whenever we produced good work in the lessons, she would stick a star in our books next to the piece in question. If the work was excellent, it would be a gold star, and these badges of excellence were greatly coveted. One day I was sitting next to her desk when the box of stars fell onto the floor, spilling its contents. I rushed to her aid, partly to earn the praise of my teacher, but also to appropriate a number of stars for personal use. When I returned home that afternoon, I proudly showed off my workbook, covered in stars of all colours, to my parents. They were less impressed than I had hoped and the following morning, before the start of lessons, my father and I went to confess the crime to Miss Fazakerley. He took pains not to humiliate me, but there was no doubt in my mind that this was an adventure not to be repeated.

Unfortunately, only a month or so later, I had forgotten the lesson that crime does not pay by stealing a small wooden tank from a toy shop in Nevill Street. My lack of any sense of guilt was exemplified by the fact that, when my mother and I went for tea and cakes at the Kardomah on Lord Street a few minutes later, I played with the toy on the table quite openly. When asked where the tank had come from, I replied, with transparent honesty, that I had seen it in the shop, had wanted it, and therefore had taken it. Sadly, my motives were not considered appropriate and so, returning to the shop, I stood sheepishly as my mother explained to the assistant that a boy had taken the tank, but he now wished to return it because he realised that it was a wrong thing to do. Quite rightly, she made sure that no presents were bought for me over

14

a period of several weeks, in the hope that my new-found appetite for acquisition would abate. It did.

My only other memory from that time involved the breaking of one of the ten commandments. When I returned home from school one day I told my mother that a boy in our class had committed adultery. "He committed adultery? How do you know," she asked, presumably suppressing a smile. "I saw it running down his leg," I replied with due seriousness. The reasoning was drawn from an answer to my question of what exactly was the meaning of 'Thou shalt not commit adultery', for I had already heard of The Ten Commandments. This was a period when I demanded detailed answers to questions, particularly those referring to words I had not previously encountered. The easy way for my parents was to tell me that adultery was something very rude. By far the rudest thing I could think of at that young age was diarrhoea, even ruder than knickers.

19431943194319431943194319431943194319431943

FRIENDS AND NEIGHBOURS

'Can Paul play?' It was Rita Dart, quite pretty, quick-speaking in a refined accent. We often played in her garden with Flora Scales who lived across the road from Rita, although quite what we did is now lost in memory. The other female friend who called to see if I could play was Margaret Irving. She was a little shy and quieter than Rita, and I married her in a full-dress ceremony in her back garden when we were both four. Like many marriages of today, it didn't last, but the cake was good. A third girl-friend was Thelma Gott, the tom-boy younger sister of David, with both of whom at a later date I played hours and hours of football on Bedford Park, often carrying on long after sunset when seeing the ball was almost impossible. The most memorable escapade with Thelma was when we decided to paint my mother's washing mangle in black enamel paint as a surprise. We undertook our work in the wash house very thoroughly, even covering the rubber rollers, yet despite that, my mother was most ungrateful and we were both punished for our thoughtful act of kindness.

Across the road lived the Exworthys. Father was headmaster of Our Lady of Lourdes School and later Christ The King School. He was also one of the few car owners in our road, running a Vauxhall Twelve. The sons were John and younger brother Peter, with whom I played from time to time. One day Peter and I decided to cut each other's hair, which we did in the privacy of the orchard down our garden, with a large pair of kitchen scissors. Although we felt really proud of our handiwork, this

15

The family home in Lyndhurst Road, Birkdale

view was not shared by our mothers, and more recrimination followed. It was, however, my father's agnosticism that caused a rift between Peter and me some weeks later. "Your father doesn't go to Mass," he accused, presumably repeating a comment he had heard at home. I did what any red-blooded six-year-old would do and pushed him backwards into the gooseberry bush. More punishment followed, although it was somewhat mitigated by the consideration that my crime had been driven by the will to defend the Bagshaw family honour. Although my father could not bring himself to believe in God, partly as a result of his reading of philosophy, he was most solicitous to find for my mother the location of the nearest Catholic church whenever the family moved house.

Other children in the road were Peter Croston, with whom I would later form a friendship when we went to King George V School at the age of eleven, Christopher Metcalfe, who occasionally played football with us, despite finding Thelma's style of play a bit rough for him, Pamela Preston and her two sisters who lived with their mother, and Alan Pearson, Billy Lloyd, Pat Karmy and Rita Dart's brother, Peter, who were too old for us to play with. Our own next-door neighbours were the Philpotts on one side and Mrs Marshall, who cooked on one of those old-fashioned ranges, on the other. Further down the road was Miss McGinnell who gave me piano lessons from the age of five. She once told my mother proudly that Peter Exworthy was going to be a priest, and wasn't that simply marvellous news, and how wonderful it was for his family. "What does Paul want to be?" she enquired. "A burglar," replied my mother without a hint of a smile, as her neighbour's jaw dropped.

A boy of my own age whom I met infrequently was Nicholas Kendall. He was the younger son of my godparents, Dick and Hilda Kendall, and from time to time they visited us from their home in Preston. We got on well as we played in the garden, but we did not meet sufficiently often to become close friends. The significance of Nicholas in my life is that, when we were both seven, he died. Aside from Rita's death three years earlier, this was my first confrontation with human mortality, and its shock was deepened by the fact that he was my own age. I was told that he died from blood poisoning - which I now imagine must have been tetanus - caused by a wound from a rusty nail. The impact of this event upon me was quite chilling, and the thought of it haunted me for several months.

There was a group of young people in their late teens in our road. My step-brother Denis, Douglas and Eileen Gaunt who lived next door but one and whose family were another of the few who had cars in their drives, in this case a Hillman, David and Connie Philpott who lived to our immediate right and whose young brother, Neil, was closer to my age, and Edna Wardle across the road. I felt sympathy for this group of people, for they didn't ever seem to have any fun. I never saw them playing out and they certainly never joined in football on Bedford Park. They probably never cut each other's hair either, although perhaps this was an experience better avoided. I pondered with some trepidation on whether or not I would become dull like them when I grew older, and gave some thought to making the best of my childhood in case my life were to follow this drift into tedium later on.

Two events that broadened my experience in 1944 were the beginning of attending and giving parties and the operation to remove my tonsils. The parties were most exciting. If you went to someone else's birthday, you took a present with you and remembered, if you could, to say 'thank you for having me' to the child's mother, who I imagine must have felt some relief at my departure. Your own parties were magnificent, for everybody brought presents for you and you had the challenge of blowing out seven candles at one go, even though your mother was probably helping you discreetly by adding to the blowing power. My own social life went into suspension briefly in that year during the removal of my tonsils. After the operation I spent several days eating nothing and sipping iced water out of a strange teapot-shaped vessel, a period of no enjoyment whatsoever. Despite my sore throat, I couldn't wait to get back to school and to rejoin the Lyndhurst Road social scene.

Unlike some neighbourhoods, ours was not one with grumpy grown-ups who wouldn't give you your ball back when it went over their wall. Mrs Marshall, in particular, exhibited a good-natured patience on the hundreds of occasions I troubled her on this pretext. The adults who did worry me were the occasional visitors to the area. Our coalmen, Walter Howard and his identical brother, were frightening to behold for a six-year-old, mainly because of their coal-black faces, flat caps, leather aprons and heavy clogs. They never did me any harm, but I was careful to keep out of the way when deliveries took place. Other delivery men and inspectors posed no threat, but I hadn't trusted the window cleaner since he wiped my face with his leather as a joke. Then there was the bogey man who was said to lurk in the air raid shelter, the damp smell of which I still recall. The man I was most anxious to avoid was the rag and bone man, for it was rumoured that he collected boys and girls as well as rags and bones. He sat on the very back edge of a two-wheeled cart drawn by a geriatric horse. I was puzzled by his regular shout of 'Bawn!'. What about the rags, I wondered, and I noticed that, even when his cart was piled high with discarded items, there was no sign of a rag or a bone amongst them. Clearly, he was not to be trusted. In conclusion, I cannot refer to terrifying figures without the mention of my dentist, Mr Highton.

Although he never did me any harm, I viewed my visits to the Clinic on the corner of Church Street with horror, even though he always gave me a cinnamon tablet after treatment. It was his huge size and his bald head that scared me witless. Forget about the Hound of the Baskervilles and Hannibal Lecter. The star of my personal horror movie was Mr Highton!

19451945194519451945194519451945194519451945

THE DEMISE OF UNCLE JACK

Jack Bagshaw was my father's younger brother. At quite an early age, probably in his twenties, Jack inherited a considerable amount of money from an elderly friend of the family and so, for much of his adult life, he had no need to work in order to live. His main passion was gambling, and he would visit us several times a year in an attempt to persuade his brother to go to the races or the dog track. My father was rather weak willed when it came to betting on almost anything, but he could not afford to keep up with his prosperous brother, as my mother knew only too well. I liked Jack for he was very jolly and friendly and, at twenty-two stone, had an enormous presence. His main asset was a beautiful baritone voice, which might well have led him to a professional career had he wished to follow that route. Denis told a different story, recalling that Jack was really a dislikeable man whose sarcasm was unpleasant and unkind. As he was much older than I, and therefore more perceptive, I must trust his judgement.

When I was about fifteen months old, Uncle Jack and my father, under the influence of quite an amount of beer whilst my mother was out shopping, brainwashed me to say 'ta' instead of thank you. Their joke was not at all appreciated by my mother on her return, particularly as the two men could not stop giggling, and it took her quite some time to reindoctrinate me. In fact, she was highly suspicious of Jack for she believed, quite rightly, that his plan was to lead my father astray, especially where money was concerned. Once, after a session of poker, Jack demanded that his brother pay him the £1,000 he had lost during the game, but he got no joy from my mother, whom he often attempted to charm, with no success at all, with flowers, chocolates and compliments on her cooking. It was inevitable that the time would come when Jack Bagshaw's money finally ran out. Twenty-five years of gambling, drinking and unsupported spending had reduced his prosperity to the level where he had to face the most unattractive prospect of all: work. At first, it looked as though his luck would hold out well, for he applied, and was called to interview, for a most interesting occupation - chauffeur to Josef Locke, the celebrated and hugely popular Irish tenor who worked

19

the summer season at Blackpool every year. Evidently, Jack was impressive at the interview, but when it came to the driving, the poor man faced an insurmountable difficulty. At over twenty stone he could not get behind the wheel, and so it was that he started work on the only other occupation freely available at that time of year, deck chair attendant. It was in this noble capacity that Jack Bagshaw became a member, albeit a reluctant one, of the working class.

When Uncle Jack was no longer fit to work, he spent most of his time as a paying guest in a small run-down Blackpool boarding house, drinking cheap wine and putting the occasional few pence on the horses, a habit he was unable to forgo. Although he outlived my father, it was only by a few years, and one day in the mid-1950s, he was found dead in bed with a bottle of wine in his hand. It was a pathetic end for a man who could have made so much more of his talents, but I suspect that he was happy for the larger part of his life. He was the archetypal naughty boy - the family's black sheep - and when he died it was with insufficient money to pay for his own funeral, and yet I remember him with affection. Both Jack and Gilbert Bagshaw were optimists, and I am eternally grateful to have inherited this life-enhancing characteristic.

MUSICAL EXPERIENCES

I started learning the piano at the age of three, taught by my father. He was an accomplished pianist with an extensive collection of bound piano manuscripts by Beethoven, Schubert, Brahms, Liszt, Schumann, Mendelssohn, Chopin, Debussy, Rachmaninov, Bartok and other celebrated composers. One year later I went to Miss McGinnell's house at number 64 to continue with piano tuition for a further four years. She was very fussy and talkative, but I did make progress, despite my preference for playing by ear rather than from the manuscript. I was just six when my father took me to my first concert, a piano recital at the Grand Theatre on Lord Street by a Russian called Poushnoff. In 1946, just before I left home for boarding school, I was taken to the Garrick Theatre to attend my very first symphony concert. It was quite spellbinding, and my main memory is of a performance of the Schumann Piano Concerto in A Minor, the effect of which stayed with me for years afterwards.

Being brought up in a household where classical music is a permanent feature is an enriching experience, and is one of the finest gifts a child can receive. It was my great good fortune that, from the age of eight, I was participating in discussions with my father about music and about composers, and we talked on what felt to me then as an equal footing of our likes and dislikes. He taught me the names of the major composers and infected me with his enthusiasms. My mother was also a music lover who played the piano whenever time allowed, and it was a great regret to both of them when a shortage of money required the selling of the Dagmar upright grand piano in 1946. Denis's main passion was jazz, which I found exotic, but was not of great interest to me otherwise. Nevertheless, I do remember the stir caused in our house by the constant playing of 'In the Mood' by the Glen Miller Band, just as I recall 'Don't sit under the Apple Tree with anyone else but me'.

Further visits to the theatre then followed. Amongst other performances, I saw two operas, 'Cavalleria Rusticana' by Mascagni and 'Faust' by Gounod, which featured the tenor, Walter Midgeley. Meanwhile, my own musical attainments remained modest, for I much preferred to play football than to spend the necessary amount of time practising the piano. So it is that, as an adult I cannot play anything particularly well, but I do have that deep love of music bestowed upon me by my father all those years ago. Just as we never forget how to swim or to ride a bicycle, we never lose our love and appreciation of the arts, and music is probably the affective of all.

INTO THE BIG SCHOOL

Being the eldest in the Infant School is not one of life's loftiest achievements, and we all longed for the day when we would move into the Juniors - the Big School. As with most promotions, and quite detached from one's level of maturity at the time, there is a bitter-sweet combination of ecstasy and sheer panic during such transitions. I was so thrilled to be in Farnborough Road Junior School I could barely contain my excitement, yet the worry of boys two, three and even four years older than myself was palpable, and placed something of a limit on my joy. Inevitably, there was the worry of bullying but, as so often happens, it was largely the fear of the unknown, for I cannot recall ever being threatened, let alone attacked - at least, not by boys. The person I was to fear most was not a child but a teacher, and that was my form mistress, Miss B. Her clear dislike of me could not be explained merely by my mischievous behaviour. I have no doubt now that she saw her authority over me as a means of scoring points off my father, her teaching colleague. To this day, I do not know what she thought might be gained by such actions as shaking me by the hair, but that is what she did. In truth, I was not the only boy so treated, but I most certainly received the sharpness of her tongue and the pain of her bony fingers on my scalp more frequently than any other child in the form. As a staff colleague, my father was not the best placed to address this problem, but he had no need to worry. My mother dealt ruthlessly with Miss B, as described later. Although the victimisations ceased, the effects of this over a long period caused nightmares and bed-wetting for some time to come, and the latter was still a problem as I started boarding school the following year.

As is often the case in Junior Schools, very few of the staff were male. The headmaster was Mr Bracewell, later succeeded by Mr Loveridge, and the only other men were my father, his good friend Mr Thomas and a young teacher, Mr Hamilton, who stayed with us for a short time until he found accommodation. I met him again nearly forty years later in the year he retired as head teacher of Westvale Primary School in Kirkby. My father was an excellent teacher who was very popular with the children, mainly because he was such a nice man. At the end of term he would read them extracts from Hugh Lofting's 'Doctor Doolittle', mimicking the voices of the animals. What they didn't know was that, when the pressure of work piled up, he would sometimes pay a teaching colleague a shilling to mark his books.

Amongst the boys I knew at that time were Peter Croston, Peter Langtree, Roy Beckett, Freddy Wilson, Tony Reuben, Robin Cheffins, Clifford Tasker, Rodney Hilton and Brian Gill, almost all of whom were to join me at King George V School three years later. However, for the very first time in my young life I started to take notice of girls, not with any strong preoccupation, but without the dismissive attitude I had previously displayed. Sylvia Rockcliffe and Gillian Wareing were frequent fellow passengers on the bus to school, and so I got to know them quite well. As ever, the girls I found most attractive were those whom I hardly knew at all. My interest was no doubt enhanced by their unfamiliarity and, in consequence, their apparent unattainability. Margaret Worsley was attractive and rather taller than I was, but this did not prevent Peter Bimpson and me from becoming rivals for her affection. Despite this, I doubt if she noticed either of us. My favourite of all was Brenda Gill, whose looks were, and still are, stunning, just like a young Elizabeth Taylor. My fascination for her almost ended in tears, mainly because of her hair. Brenda had short dark brown hair in what was called a page-boy style. It stuck out at the back and I was intrigued to know whether this protrusion was hair or head. Because I sat behind her in class, I could not resist the temptation one morning to poke a pencil into the mysterious region. To my horror and to her pain, I discovered that it was head, and I was very lucky that Brenda Gill was ever again prepared to speak to me. In fact we were to become art students together in the 1950s, by which time all had been forgiven, if not quite forgotten.

Despite the comradeship of fellow pupils at school, my main friends remained those who lived nearby and who were accessible during leisure hours. One major event we all experienced was the celebration of VE Day, marking the end of the Second World War in Europe, hostilities

Farnborough Road School

My father (left) with his Farnborough Road School colleagues

23

with Japan remaining until the atom bombs were dropped on Hiroshima and Nagasaki later in the year. Like almost every part of the country we organised street parties and hoisted union jack flags - in our case a red ensign on a clothes prop - outside our houses. The ceremony for my own age group involved a trip around the area on Walter Howard's coal cart followed by a high tea at a long table located in the drive of Whiteley's Laundry on Clifford Road. We all sat there wearing home made paper hats, eating spam sandwiches, sponge fancies and blancmange, and drinking unbearably strong tea that left a brown skin on your upper lip, all to the encouraging smiles and promptings of the kindly silver-haired ladies who had organised the event. I imagine that, in view of the severities of rationing in those days, putting on such a tea party required considerable ingenuity and sacrifice on their part. Such was the relief amongst the adult community that nobody counted the cost.

Some time early in 1946 there was a discussion in our house about my educational future. The outcome was that I should move in the following September to Alderwasley Hall, a boys' preparatory school in the depths of the Derbyshire countryside. I can recall no strong views of my own about the pros and cons of such a change, and I was later told that the decision was driven by my father's belief that only children - my step-brother being fourteen years older than I - were in danger of being over-mothered and that a boarding education would also give me a stronger sense of independence and self-reliance. My sister-in-law tells me that at least part of the motivation behind this plan was the need to find suitable accommodation for Great Aunt Lucy at our house. I have no way of evaluating the relative strengths of these influences over my future, but it is worth noting that Lucy paid for three years of boarding for me, a task that my parents could not possibly have afforded. Auntie Lucy and I were good friends, and we spent much time asking each other ingenious riddles and laughing at the answers. Our relationship flourished in a manner that often occurs between those whose ages are separated by two generations and I think we both missed each other when I moved to Alderwasley. So it was that, in the middle of 1946, I left Farnborough Road School, and I left Southport, to embark on a new venture in the independent sector, completely unaware of what the future might bring. I now find it surprising that I remember neither sadness at leaving one school nor apprehension at joining another. Either I have forgotten the feelings I experienced, or I must conclude that, at the age of eight, children just accept life as it is. If that is so, perhaps it is just as well. My major worry was whether or not, during my absence, my white mice would be cared for in a manner to which they had both become accustomed. They weren't.

PART TWO
PREP SCHOOL DAYS
1946-1949

194619461946194619461946194619461946

THE FIRST DAY

My parents took me for an interview to Alderwasley Hall Prep School in summer, 1946. Although I recall very little of the events of that day, I have not forgotten our encounter with wild animals on the way. When we arrived at Whatstandwell Station we decided to walk up to the school, unaware of the distance and the terrain. This involved walking about two miles, half of which was across pasture populated by a herd of Friesians. Mr father's fear of cows, although irrational, was real, and it says much for his courage that we persevered with our route.

I was accepted for Alderwasley and, on the first day of the Autumn term, my mother escorted me on the train from Southport to Manchester Victoria, from where we took a taxi across the city to Central Station. Having spotted a few other boys with blue caps bearing the silver unicorn badge of Alderwasley Hall, I made her promise not to kiss me, a promise she made and promptly broke in a flood of emotion prompted by my imminent departure for Derbyshire. She never really came to terms with my leaving home, and this was just another example. I was eight years old and could well do without such embarrassing displays of affection, but I bore the indignity with stoicism, whilst receiving the encouragement of understanding looks from my new-found companions. They had evidently suffered similar maternal excesses.

25

There were six of us in the carriage, all of the same age. Rodney Bell came from Preston. He was tall with red hair and, throughout our time at the school, I was destined always to come second in end-of-term examinations behind him. James Ayling was small and serious, and Tony Campbell, a chemist's son from Wigan, was plump with a black fringe and fat, red cheeks. Others were Anthony Fazakerley, whose father was a dentist in Wallasey, and Patrick Smyth, the son of an Irish doctor from Atherton and a keen Manchester United supporter, a cause to which he very soon converted me. Fazakerley, Smyth and I became firm friends for our entire boarding school careers.

We chatted excitedly on the train journey, picking up more boys at Stockport, Chinley, Miller's Dale and Matlock. At Whatstandwell there was a coach to transport us, along with quite a number of local boys, up the hill to Alderwasley. Mr Reilly, a Scotsman who was soon to become my favourite teacher, took charge of the operation. On arrival at the back of the main school building, we alighted from the coach with joyful anticipation tinged with the inevitable fear of the unknown. The first step was to allocate us to dormitories, and we clattered up stairs carrying a few essentials from our large cabin trunks.

My own dormitory was St Luke's, which I shared with Ayling, Bell, Ryan along with two seven-year-olds that we always referred to as 'babes'. As soon as we had unpacked, we were given tea in the Dining Hall before being taken on a tour of the grounds. A particular feature of interest was a series of four pools, each feeding the next with water from a cascade at the top of the first. I leaned over the edge of the lowest pool to see if there were any fish and, to everyone's surprise including my own, I fell in. This was the first of many occasions when I witnessed the angry and impatient look of Mr James, my new Headmaster. I was sent straight to Matron for drying off and changing, and the rest of the day left me in a slightly subdued frame of mind.

We went to bed at about 7.45 pm with an instruction not to talk after lights out. Like most boys of that age, we proved incapable of keeping the rule, imagining that nobody would hear our whispers. We were mistaken. The door was opened authoritatively before the squelching sound of Mr James' crepe soles filled the room. "I heard talking!" he barked. "Who was talking?" I had been brought up to believe that owning up was the right thing to do, and spared you from worse punishment than the concealing of the truth. "I was talking, Mr James," I volunteered. No-one else said a word. They were either less naive or more afraid than I. The Headmaster told me to stand at the end of my bed and left the room. I could feel the sickness in my stomach, although I had no idea what he'd planned to do. A few minutes later, he

The author, aged eight, with his parents

returned with a cane. "Bend over the end of the bed," he ordered. I complied, wearing only a dressing gown. I was given four strokes on my behind, administered with some force. I cried myself to sleep on that very first night, not only with the pain, but also from a burning sense of injustice. My punishment, it would appear, took no account whatsoever of my naive honesty.

LISTS AND TIMETABLES

Most boarders travelled with trunks rather than suitcases, mainly because of the huge amount of clothing required for the coming term. In addition to the requirements for every garment to carry names tapes, our school number had to be marked on more or less everything we possessed, including shoes. Mine bore a number made up of small brass nails hammered into the sole. I had a coat hook on the games corridor bearing the number 19, which would remain with me for the rest of my stay.

CLOTHING LIST

Req.	ARTICLES	Req.	ARTICLES
1*	School Blazer	1*	School Cap
1	Grey shorts or long trousers (best)	1*	School Tie
		1	Cricket sweater
2*	Grey roll-neck jerseys	1	V-neck pullover (sleeveless)
2	Grey shorts (hardwearing)	1	Pair Cricket whites (long or short)
2	Pairs of shoes		
1	Pair of plimsolls	2*	Football stockings
1	Pair of wellingtons	1	Pair football shorts
3	Grey shirts with collars attached		
2	Grey Aertex shirts (Summer)	2*	Football jerseys (Blue and badge)
5	Pairs grey stockings (with mending wool)	1	Pair football boots
		3	Bath towels (with hanging loops)
3	Vests		
3	Pairs of pants	1	Bathing costume
3	Pyjama suits	2	Boot brushes & polish
1	Dozen handkerchieves	1	Shoe bag (18" square)
1	Dressing gown		Toilet requisites
1	Pair of slippers		(brushes, comb,
2	Belts		face cloths,
			toothbrush, soap,
			toothpaste)

Each article of clothing must be clearly marked with the boy's Christian name and surname, in Cash's name tapes, not with stick-on tapes. Shoes and boots must also be clearly marked. All articles marked (*) should be obtained from the School's official outfitter: Gorringes of London.

The school day worked to a regular timetable. After rising, washing in cold water and dressing, we were all expected to walk or run the Morning Round, a distance of just over half a mile round the outside of the main school buildings. In the evening, bath times were either in the Mayflower with Matron, Mrs Babbage, or in the Ark Royal with Sister, Miss Clay. The advantage of the former was that Matron told us of the film she had seen at the cinema in Derby earlier in the week. It was a rare contact with normal life, for we heard no radio, saw no newspapers or comics, visited no shops and spent no money.

DAILY TIMETABLE

7.00	Rise - Wash - Dress - Morning Round
7.30	Mass in the Chapel
8.15	Breakfast in Dining Hall
8.45	Bed-making and shoe inspection
9.00	Prep
9.30	Lesson 1
10.15	Lesson 2
11.00	Morning break - Tuck Shop
11.30	Lesson 3
12.15	Lesson 4
1.00	Lunch in Dining Hall
1.30	Chapel visit - Quiet period (Reading or writing letters)
2.00	Free time
2.30	Games or Walk
4.00	Tea in Dining Hall
4.30	Prep
5.00	Lesson 5
5.45	Lesson 6
6.30	Prep
7.00	Supper in Dining Hall
7.20	Free time - Clubs or stories
7.45	Junior bedtime - Baths on alternate nights
8.45	Senior bedtime - Baths on alternate nights
9.10	Lights out

FOOD, GLORIOUS FOOD

If I describe the food at Alderwasley as basic, I must allow for the fact that I am recalling a period immediately after the end of the war. Breakfast provided either khaki-coloured corn flakes or mid-grey porridge, which set like a jelly and floated on top of the milk, but contained oat husks which we called 'toe-nails'. We had dry bread and bacon, cooked so insufficiently that the fat was soft and translucent. My own particular weakness, then and now, is that I am unable to eat any kind of soft fat without vomiting. When one particular breakfast had ended and I started to leave the table with soft bacon fat still on my plate, I was reprimanded by my Form Mistress, Miss Barr, who told me that there were starving children in the world who would be glad of my leavings and that I must eat it up at once. Despite my warning that I would be sick, she remained insistent that I should eat the fat between two doorsteps of bread. Her mistake was in sitting next to me whilst I attempted to swallow the greasy breakfast residue. True to my prediction, I vomited my entire breakfast, including the porridge, all over her brown Harris Tweed skirt.

Other foods I found quite distasteful were fish, which I covered with pepper to disguise the taste, cabbage, which I once vomited at my first (and only) appearance on top table as one of the more senior boys, and sprouts, for which I devised a most ingenious plan. In order to make sure that we opened our bowels regularly, Matron would stand outside the lavatories with a clip-board onto which she recorded our movements. As each boy left the cubicle he would say "Yes, Matron", indicating that the visit had been successful, or "No, Matron", signifying failure. Whenever we had sprouts I would put them in the breast pocket of my grey shirt and, on my next visit to the lavatory, drop them from a height into the basin, pull the chain and say "Yes, Matron", after leaving the cubicle. This not only got rid of the sprouts, but also enabled me to avoid California Syrup of Figs issued to the constipated amongst us or, even worse, Cascara Evacuant for the very seriously blocked-up. Goodness knows what my shirt must have smelled like after this regular ritual, but I was proud of the ingenuity of my plan to kill two birds with one stone, whereby I could avoid both sprouts and constipation treatment at a stroke.

The most exciting food by far was the tuck we brought with us at the beginning of each term, and which we could draw upon in limited quantities at morning break each day. The greedy ones, who wolfed their rations and had nothing left with weeks to go, queued up in the corridor to beg from those whose forward planning had been more accurate. "Gi'us a sweet!" was the plaintive cry. Tuck was also a strong bargaining counter, for you could borrow someone's water pistol for half an hour for the swap of a piece of iced fruit cake, even if it was buried in the pockets of your corduroy shorts for three days, along with a metal puzzle, three marbles and a handkerchief. Chocolate Spread was popular, but the ultimate delicacy was peanut butter, which Michael Holbrook had sent to him regularly from America. His bouts of acceptability appeared to coincide with the arrival of these food parcels, and to disappear when all the peanut butter had been consumed.

BOYS FROM EVERYWHERE

Apart from Stephen Deville, who lived only a hundred yards from the school, all boys were boarders, even those who lived within travelling distance, like Brian Ibberson from Matlock. Most came from some distance; John Ryan from Exeter, brothers Francis and Anthony Percival from St Albans, Henry Mumford-Smith from Ireland, Nicholas Armstrong from somewhere in Scotland, and a number of us from Lancashire. The only strong accents I can remember were those of David Fox, and his brother Bill, who stammered, both from Sheffield, and the Nottingham contingent of Nigel and Philip Murphy, Mark Flanagan, Charles Holmes and Nicholas Martin. Harry Trindall could not say 'sh', so my name became 'Bagsaw'. "He's got a bone in his nose", explained John Babbage. "Oh," we said.

Some pupils came from overseas, mainly as a result of families fleeing from the Nazi threat during the Second World War. The first I met was a shy French boy named Léon Tibergien. I can see now his continental-style jacket that had a half-belt design incorporated into the waistline at the back. This appeared most eccentric to my conservative mind. His receding chin and forehead and his hairstyle made him look very like a young King George VI. The angular featured Albert Steigler came from Austria, and Meinhardt and Skorski were German Jews. The largest foreign contingent was from Poland - Ferenc Prugar, whose wore a pin-striped navy blue suit with shorts that had turn-ups on them, the very clever Roman Beldowski, Andrzej Morawicz who resembled Danny Kaye and, finally, Oswaldo Roswadowski, known as 'Ossie Odd-Socks' for reasons that are probably self-evident..

All of these boys, without exception, were more mature than we were and worked much more diligently. I imagine that they had a more highly developed consciousness of the need to prepare for a successful adult life, in view of their traumatised childhood. The Polish boys had greater self-assurance than the others from abroad, largely because four are able to develop a greater camaraderie than one or two. However, they integrated well with the rest of us and were generally popular.

31

Waiting for a run at the front of Alderwasley Hall

The extremes of winter in 1947

The boy whom we liked best was Loreto Scala, a swarthy Italian. He was full of fun, friendly in a rather demonstrative way and, of particular importance in a boarding school, a good fighter. He joined in with Tony Fazakerley, Patrick Smyth and myself as part of a happy and rather mischievous quartet. One boy, I think it was Miles Hodgetts, enjoyed a period of great popularity when he became the very first in the school to own a biro, which had been invented only about a year previously. It had been sent to him from America and, although it leaked furiously onto paper, fingers and clothing, to all of us it represented the glamour of future technology. The refills were hopeless for they had no ball-point on the end, and were just tubes of ink that had to be pushed onto the writing section with disastrous results. Despite this, we all would have died for one of our own.

194719471947194719471947194719471947

TEACHERS AND LESSONS

My first form teacher was Katharine Barr. She was plump and tweedy, with the almost obligatory twin set and pearls. We were made to work hard, which is both appropriate and admirable, but I do not recall much laughter in our lessons. Almost daily, my own attempts to amuse my form-mates were met with the reprimand, "Bagshaw! Don't look round for approbation!", in the style of Lady Bracknell. Her own vocabulary made hardly any concessions to our eight-year-old level of understanding, but I suppose it is arguable that this is the best way to stretch intelligent youngsters. Despite this, the utter complexity of 'Parts of Speech', such as onomatopoeia, was of dubious value to us at that stage, although it must be admitted that we ended up understanding this, and the other related concepts, by the time she had finished. Fragments of her examples are still deep in my memory. "The camel is the ship of the desert," she proclaimed, to convey the idea of metaphor to us. "The camel is the ship of the desert," we responded obediently. "Hyperbole," announced Miss Barr with all the thespian grandeur of a veteran pantomime dame, "is overdue exaggeration". "What is hyperbole, everyone?" "Hyperbole is overdue exaggeration, Miss Barr," we chorused. She also taught me the piano, but I recall that she was irritated by my insistence on playing by ear, rather than by manuscript.

Mr Wilkinson lived with his wife at the Bothy in the grounds of the school. He was generally popular, but had an unattractive habit - one that he shared with the Headmaster - of screwing up his face in annoyance and staring demonically at whichever boy had annoyed him. Sometimes, you were to experience this stare for what seemed to be a full minute before you found out what you had done wrong. Despite this, we generally enjoyed his English, French and Maths lessons, and we were particularly fond, if a little apprehensive, of his alsatian, Sally. When she later gave birth to eight pups, we were delirious with excitement, and so were they. Like Mr Reilly, he took us on enjoyable country walks, and we were infected by his obvious love of the outdoors. He also directed a musical, the title of which now escapes me, in which I had the leading role.

Mr Reilly was unusual because he was an albino, having white wavy hair, white eyebrows and pink eyes. I remember once asking Miss Barr why his eyes were pink, to which she replied, "Don't be so silly! Mr Reilly's eyes are blue!" This was plainly untrue and was, to us, further evidence that she fancied him. He was undoubtedly the most popular of all who taught us, for he seemed to understand the schoolboy mind in a way that the others didn't and, although he could be extremely strict when necessary, he was generally even-tempered. His lowland Scottish accent made him interesting to learn from and, above all, he had a sense of humour. One of our great treats on winter evenings was to sit round a huge log fire whilst Mr Reilly read 'Just William' or 'Billy Bunter' to us. The sad side of Andrew Reilly was that he lived in a rather decrepit caravan in the school grounds, making his own meals and spending much time on his own. I later discovered, on a visit to see him in the late 1960s, that this was partly due to an unresolved dispute with the Head over pay, but he did not elaborate. This clarified, to some extent, an occurrence in 1948 when, to our surprise and horror, Mr Reilly left the school. We learned of this only on our arrival at Whatstandwell Station at the beginning of a new term, when we were met by a new teacher, Mr Reid-Smith. He may well have been a nice enough man, but he had none of his predecessor's charisma. Exactly one term later, Mr Reilly returned to a tumultuous welcome, and it is clear that whatever financial dispute had occurred was now resolved.

John James was, as Headmaster, more remote than his colleagues, yet there was evidence of kindness in his manner. Although he did not give verbal praise too frequently, his comments on my reports were invariably generous and encouraging, and he predicted a strong academic future for me. He taught us Latin, History and Religion, and much of the latter was concerned with the learning of the Catechism. *"Who made you?"* was an easy enough question to answer, but *"What has God prepared for those who love him?"* was a different matter altogether. The effectiveness of the teaching, coupled with the great fear of getting it wrong, has equipped me today to respond: *"Eye has not seen, nor has ear heard, nor has it entered into the heart of man to know what God has prepared for those who love him."* It sounds a little like a complex way of saying "We don't know". It was one of the answers I remember learning just before a number of us were confirmed by the Bishop of Nottingham, for we had been warned that he would ask questions of some of us. I was lucky enough to be overlooked on that occasion and so, with no doctrinal interrogation, I emerged the proud owner of a new confirmation name - Michael - which gave me the opportunity to write P.D.M.Bagshaw on everything that I possessed.

I think my favourite subject at the age of ten was Latin. With its case endings, it appealed to me - just as the logic of Maths did - rather than as a means of communication. It was taught by the Head, and so we all paid the fullest attention for every minute of the lesson. Despite his relative formality, John James also read stories to us on winter evenings, but the book he chose, 'Bevis', was not to us remotely as exciting as William Brown or stories from Greyfriars, mainly because Bevis never seemed to do anything exciting, like eating other people's cherry cake or scowling at old ladies. As a grown-up, I have concluded that the Headmaster's motivation in starting Alderwasley towards the end of the war was one of idealism, for I sense that he had a genuine belief in the value for young boys of a traditional residential education in a rural setting. He had a wife who was bed-ridden and whom we rarely saw. As far as we were aware, he had no children of his own. A year after I left, and at the death of his wife, he sold Alderwasley Hall to the Benedictines, who made it a prep school for Belmont, and he then entered a monastic order.

SPECIAL DORMITORIES

Two dormitories differed from the rest because they catered for those with medical problems. St Alban's was reserved for the bed-wetters, of whom I was one in the early part of my Alderwasley career. The problem had started at Farnborough Road Junior School, where my form Teacher, Miss B, had terrorised me to the point where my mother went to the school, confronted her, and promised to report her to the Chief Education Officer if her vindictive behaviour did not cease forthwith. My father was a teacher at the same school, but he was clearly in a weaker position than my mother to deal with a problem that involved one of his colleagues. Even though the difficulty was sorted out, I clearly bore the emotional tension for some time, for my bed-wetting persisted for a term at my new school. We all had rubber sheets on our beds, and bore the responsibility of taking our wet bedding to the laundry before breakfast. It was a despairing experience, but one which, thankfully, was not a permanent one.

St Roc, the other dormitory located on the third floor of the building, was reserved for those suffering from whatever infectious disease happened to be prevalent at the time. Sometimes it was measles; on other occasions it was whooping cough. In my case it was mumps, and we 'mumpites' were isolated in this dormitory on the third floor overlooking the school yard. We took no part in lessons and were able to read books, eat sweets and tell each other rude jokes to our hearts' content. All our meals were delivered on trays, but these were frugal in the extreme. No-one bothered to supervise our washing, bed making, shoe cleaning or talking after lights out so, apart from the swollen faces, it was sheer paradise, and all boys were disappointed when they were judged to have recovered from the complaint. Against all good medical practice, we dropped sickly contaminated sweets from our lofty vantage point to our healthy compatriots below. No doubt it was impossible to stop the spread of these infections at a boarding school in any case, but our cheerful disregard of sensible behaviour did nothing at all to help the situation. Mumps, like measles, swept round the school at great speed, and we each had our turn of looking like hamsters or leopards.

MANY HAPPY RETURNS

On one occasion, my parents decided to accompany me on the journey to boarding school at the beginning of the forthcoming term. After the two train journeys, we alighted at Whatstandwell Station and, rather extravagantly, took a taxi up the hill to Alderwasley Hall. On arrival we were greeted by the Headmaster, Mr James, who took us into the reception lounge, a privileged area reserved for parents, visiting dignitaries and those about to be expelled. He assured my mother and father what a well-brought-up boy I was, what very good manners I displayed, and how well my work was progressing, despite my tendency to talk too much and to crack jokes at rather inappropriate moments, characteristics which clearly have never quite disappeared. We drank strong tea in china cups and smiled a lot, particularly the Headmaster who, as far as my experience went, did not smile too readily in the normal course of events. It wasn't until my mother and father prepared to leave that Mr James expressed surprise that we had returned back from the holiday four days early, rather than at the start of the next term. I was absolutely mortified. Much as I enjoyed school, the revelation that I had surrendered four whole days of holiday was almost too horrifying to contemplate. "Well, Paul, what would you like to do?" asked my Headmaster. "would you like to go back home now with your parents or would you like to remain here at School with us?" To this very day, I do not know what possessed me to reply "I'll stay here with you, Mr James".

It was partly the way he had phrased the question, but mainly because I thought it might sound rude if I declined his offer of four days extra hospitality. No doubt I had been far too well brought up, being anxious to appear courteous and co-operative at all times.

My parents smiled, in a way that revealed their surprise at my response, although they did not recognise my unspoken urge to reverse my decision. They were pleased to accept a lift from Matron back to the station, and I watched the car disappearing down the road with mounting emotion. I could feel tears burning inside me. Why had I said what I'd said? I regretted it even before I reached the end of the sentence. I could blame no-one for this. Why wasn't it possible to re-run the dialogue with a different outcome? I rehearsed and re-rehearsed alternative versions of the conversation, but to no avail. I was the author of my own misfortune, and a misfortune it was indeed, for the only schoolboy companions I would have for those four tamely-surrendered days were Edward Turton and Stephen Deville.

Turton, Matron's nephew, was six, and Deville, known as 'Piglet' because he looked like one, was seven. I was nine, and so I faced the prospect of the four extra days in the company of two infants with unrelieved dismay. Playing football with them was no fun at all, mainly because Turton was a wimp who was desperate to avoid physical contact at all costs, and Deville was not sufficiently co-ordinated to kick the ball in anything other than a random direction. Building dens was no better because they relied upon me to make all the decisions, as the mature member of the trio. It was my first experience of running a play group and I was not enjoying it. I went and laid on my bed to contemplate my ghastly error in solitude. My mood progressed to a level of anguish that only self-pity of the most indulgent and deeply enjoyable kind can create.

THE 1947 WINTER

By any standards, the 1947 winter was severe and, in a county such as Derbyshire, the effects were spectacular. The School was cut off from the outside world on several occasions, and one half-term was so deeply snow-bound that many boys had to remain at Alderwasley instead of spending a week at home. Some of the drifts were over ten feet deep, and it is hard to imagine an ecstasy greater than that we all experienced during this period. The only boys who did not feel unrelieved contentment were those suffering from chilblains, a condition rarely heard of today, but which seemed quite common back in the 1940s. The deep carpet of snow seemed to last, like our delight, for ever and ever, and life could hardly have been better.

Although sports like football were generally unplayable during this period, the afternoon walks continued, and the increase in potential risk of hazard and injury only heightened our enjoyment. We stepped into the footprints of the boy in front, but there were many times when the snow was so deep that we had to retrace our steps or take an alternative route. The Morning Round itself had never been so popular, but because we all exploited the event for snowball fights, we were not allowed to go unsupervised as long as the snow prevailed. An additional bonus was that the four ornamental lakes were completely frozen over with ice so thick that there was no chance at all of it cracking under our weight. So frequent were these outdoor excursions that most Alderwasley boys soaked their clothes faster than they could be dried, and many had to attend lessons dressed in a strange combination of pyjamas and sports kit.

Amidst all this activity, one experience stood out from the rest as the pinnacle of adrenalin-rushing entertainment - sledging. The school possessed a number of sledges, ranging from single-seaters to larger models carrying four and, in one case, six persons. The local boys sent messages home for more to be sent in, and instead of our routine games sessions, we took part in hair-raising sledge races. Alderwasley Hall was built on a hill, and so the terrain was quite perfect for our purposes. There were clear runs in several directions, but there were hazards. One was the stream at the bottom of the hill, but this was only a minor problem because only the six-seater fully loaded was likely to travel that distance. Far more threatening were the sawn-off tree stumps, lying like land mines under the drifting snow, and completely hidden from view. Nigel Murphy hit one of these hazards at full speed and, although his sledge stopped dead, he carried on travelling for a further ten yards or so. Another casualty was Bill Fox, whose stammer became twice as bad as usual during his agitated attempt to talk us through the accident.

Eventually, disappointment came when the snow began to recede as the temperature rose but, fortunately, it was a gradual process, and there were nearly always some frozen residues in the vicinity for us to throw at each other. Then, one morning, to the utter dismay of the entire school, it had all disappeared. The sense of anti-climax was palpable, and we began to realise how mundane everyday life really was without the diversion of extreme weather conditions. We feared that those moments would never again return and, in one sense, we were right, for comparable conditions were not to be repeated until 1963, when we were all in our twenties and far less capable of exploiting them on such a level of exultation.

MEANWHILE, BACK IN SOUTHPORT

My life during the school holidays was in strong contrast to the environment at Alderwasley. As the only child in the household - Denis being in his mid-twenties and soon to be married - I was forced to make a lot of my own entertainment, but this was never a serious problem and, as at present, the days were never long enough to complete all my projects. Our garden was generally wild and was ideal for the building of dens, a skill I had developed at boarding school. We had an orchard of sorts, but most of the fruit was inedible, being either bitter-tasting or hard as a rock. At ten, I was too old for a tricycle or a pedal car, but not yet the owner of a bike. At five you can play with girls, just as you can at fifteen, but at ten it is strictly off the agenda. Still, there was Smokey the cat, who probably had my white mice while I was away, and Auntie Lucy to play tricks on. I did join the Cubs, but stayed for only three days because the biscuits were stale. It was, perhaps, a rather hasty decision.

One of the great joys of being at home was the ability to listen to the radio, which we simply never did at school, and my firm favourite was Dick Barton - Special Agent, broadcast on the Light Programme from 6.45 to 7 each weekday evening. On Saturday morning there was the chance to listen to an hour and a quarter of the omnibus edition, keeping me abreast of the gripping adventures of Dick, Snowy and Jock. Other popular radio programmes of the period which I enjoyed were Family Favourites, introduced by Cliff Michelmore and Jean Metcalfe, Workers' Playtime, 'Have a Go' with Wilfred Pickles, and ITMA starring the country's number one comedian, Tommy Handley. Although much of its content was too grown-up for me, I remember well being intrigued by the sound of traffic at the beginning of 'In Town Tonight', an evening newsreel programme.

Going into Southport was quite exciting, particularly because we hardly ever had money at Alderwasley or, if we had, nowhere to spend it. Lord Street was really quite breathtaking with wide pavements, crowds of people, large trees, fountains, a bandstand and shops of every kind. I recall arranging to meet my mother in Thom's Tea House and, whilst waiting, I placed an order for five toasted teacakes, one for her and four for me. The perceptive waitress brought two and, in truth, I struggled to eat one and a half. This was just one of the many cafés on Lord Street - Woodhead's, the Kardomah, Matti & Tissot, Rowntree's and Sissons - but my mother's favourite was in Marshall & Snelgrove, where the fashionable women of the town met for morning coffee and for gossip, where Debenham's store is presently located. Another attractive

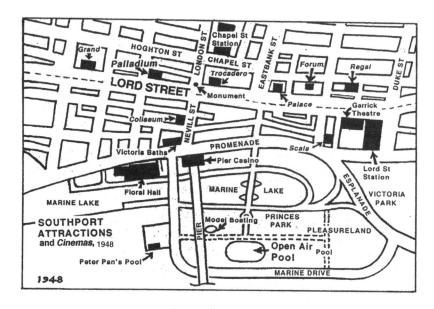

Cinemas and other Southport attractions in 1948

Nevill Street and Alexander's corner

venue was the Farmhouse Café in the Wayfarers Arcade where a four piece string ensemble played on a strange bridge-like structure suspended across the width of the arcade.

In contrast to today, the town was exceedingly well off for cinemas. The present ABC was called The Palace and, on the same side of Lord Street looking west, were the Forum, now Forum Court, and the Regal, now flats on the corner of Lord Street and Wellington Street. In the other direction were the Trocadero, demolished to make way for Woolworth's, and the Palladium, renamed Gaumont and Odeon, where Sainsbury currently stands. Further on was the Grand, now a casino. Most unfortunately, the splendid Art Deco Garrick Theatre became the Essoldo cinema, but not until later, and is now a bingo hall. The other two were the Coliseum on Nevill Street and the Scala, also a theatre for the Southport Repertory Company, on the site of the B & M car park.

In the north of the town were the Queen's and the Regent, whilst in Ainsdale was the Plaza, later to become the Moulin Rouge, then Tiffany's and, at present, a licensed restaurant. My own local cinema was the Bedford, currently a service garage, which was only about five minutes walk across the park, and you could buy Peter's chocolate, an appetising dark confection, from the little shop next door. Over the years, Peter Croston and I saw many Westerns and Abbott and Costello films in there, preceded by episodes of The Three Stooges. The two films which had the strongest effect upon me were 'The Scarlet Claw' and 'The Pearl of Death', both featuring Basil Rathbone as Sherlock Holmes and Nigel Bruce as Doctor Watson. Adults are able to retain an aesthetic distance from disturbing art forms, but children never are, and so my empathy with the horror was real and tangible. If we love to be scared, it may be a satisfaction savoured only in retrospect. Looking back, I am surprised we were considered old enough to see thrillers such as this, so perhaps we were accompanied by an adult. It was certainly much stronger stuff than my favourite reading at that time, 'Emil and the Detectives'.

Probably the most dramatic experience of 1948 for me was seeing television for the first time. My brother Denis had managed to buy a cathode ray tube shortly after being demobbed from the RAF in the previous year. As a technological wizard, he managed to set it up to receive television transmissions from Sutton Coldfield in the midlands, and we all gathered round his bench in the garage to marvel at the green, five inch, grainy picture. He was supposed to have been the first in Southport to achieve this feat, but I have no means of knowing how true that is. Either way, it was an indication of his talent for, after a period in servicing with Life's Radio in London Street, he eventually worked for the Ministry of Defence. I know of nobody who has had mains voltage through his body more than Denis, and I deduce that, over the years, he must have developed a self-preserving tolerance to 240 volts.

For those three years in the late 1940s, Southport was simply a holiday base for me, but a pleasant one. My parents didn't seem to go away very often, but I was fortunate to live in a town were there was plenty to do, even though much of it, like Pleasureland, involved spending money. The Pier was a strong attraction in those post-war days, and I recall that Billy Scott Coomber produced shows in the Pier Theatre, even though I have no recollection of seeing any of them. One of the best bargains was rowing, and there was a choice of the Marine Lake, where the boats were streamlined, or the Botanic Gardens, where they were slower and broader in shape, although much cheaper. Another venue for boating was the lake next to The Sands at Ainsdale, where the canoes had a more adventurous character. The Model Boating Lake in Princes Park was the best of all for it cost nothing and gave me the chance to sail my own boat and to look at very expensive craft built by grown-ups. As a younger child I frequented Peter Pan's Pool where they had small petrol-driven cars which were great fun to drive. My cousin Ian went boating there one day and informed us that he had sailed on 'Calamighty Jane'. Much as I enjoyed these vacations, I was pleased to get back to school, and I conclude that the available company of those of my own age was the principal attraction.

CLOSE RELATIONSHIPS

Friendships are the life-blood of boarding education but, although separate groups are formed, no-one is left out, particularly in a small school like Alderwasley. The most obvious criterion for grouping is that of age, and it was most probably to counteract this polarising that dormitories were populated by boys drawn from different years, with the exception of the very youngest who were kept together. Some friendships were based on sporting prowess, whilst others were determined by interest in particular hobbies. Yet others were the result of the most daring, or the most timid, being drawn together by personality similarities. On a temporary basis, even the bed-wetters developed a strange camaraderie born of facing a common enemy, albeit one that dare not speak its name.

Some boys who do not make friends too easily, or who arrive at school at a later date when friendship groups have already been established, try unconventional ways of being accepted. Ivor Roberts went unnoticed for two weeks after his arrival until he performed a clean vault over the school gates at the beginning of one of our afternoon walks.

Nobody had ever attempted, let alone achieved, this spectacular feat before, and Ivor gained immediate acceptance as a result. A boy called Noel, who also arrived halfway through a term, clearly felt that his name was a barrier to full integration and so, for three or four days, he persuaded us all that he was Michael King, a strategy that was quite obviously unsustainable for more than a short period.

Another form of relationship which, at the age of ten, was outside my experience was that between older and younger boys. I suppose I was vaguely aware of a number of friendships in the school between 13-year-olds and ten-year-olds who walked around together at break and lunchtime with the older boy's arm protectively round the younger boy's shoulder. Nevertheless, it did not reach my own level of consciousness until, one day, a boy called David approached me and offered protection if anyone should threaten or bully me. I was rather grateful, for David was well-built and well able to deter any unwanted aggression, although I must say that there was no-one of whom I was particularly wary.

When I look back on those days, I have to say that there was nothing sinister in the relationships described. I imagine that most of the older boys were approaching readiness for interest in girls and, in their absence, indulged their protective affections on younger boys. Despite the widely held view that boys' boarding schools were hot-beds of rampant homosexuality - and, no doubt, some of them were - ours was not one of them, and my personal recollection of these friendships is that they were entirely innocent and unconsummated. The only quasi-sexual encounter I can recall was when, at the age of ten, I stayed with my friend Brian and his family at the Central Café in Matlock. One night, before we went to sleep, Brian and I examined his pubic hair. I was somewhat envious, because I had nothing comparable, but our main interest was just one of amused curiosity, with no hint whatsoever of sexual gratification.

SPIRITUAL ENCOUNTERS

Because Alderwasley was a prep school for Catholic boys, we attended Mass every morning before breakfast. The only non-Catholic I can remember was Ivor Roberts, and I recall feeling so sorry that such a popular member of our friendship group had the grave misfortune to be a Protestant. How unlucky he was, I reflected, yet it really wasn't his fault at all. Despite this, he always joined the rest of us in worship with apparent willingness, and my childish feeling of regret at his membership of a reformist branch of Christianity was soon forgotten.

Before Mass, we lined up in a long corridor leading to the chapel, Cantoris on the left and Decani on the right. These two groupings proved ideal for the purpose of rivalry and any other situation where a polarisation of opinions was appropriate. "Decs, Decs, break their necks!" chanted the Cantoris. "Cants, Cants wet their pants!" retorted the Decani. "I'd rather break my neck than wet my pants!" shouted Nicholas Martin who, like me, was a staunch Decani, although not to my knowledge a reformed bed-wetter. Silence fell as the Headmaster appeared at the end of the corridor. He would wait for absolute quiet before indicating, with a weary arm gesture, that we should proceed. Each boy entered the small chapel, dipping two fingers onto the sponge soaked in holy water for the making of the Sign of the Cross.

Daily Mass was a simple ceremony with no singing. On Sunday it was a High Mass, with the Head at the harmonium. We wore grey flannel suits with the school badge on the breast, rather than our weekday grey shirts and corduroy shorts. Kennedy always wore long trousers, and we assumed that this signified some leg problem too horrific for others to see. The other difference on Sunday was the collection. As we lined up in the corridor, the Head came round with a bagful of money for us to put in the plate during Mass. We could ask for tuppence, in which case he gave us two pennies, or threepence, for which we received a threepenny-bit. The trick was to ask for tuppence, but to place only one of the two coins, carefully hidden under the hand, onto the plate. He must have eventually noted some discrepancy between the outgoings and the incomings for, quite suddenly one Sunday, the choice was withdrawn and we were all issued with threepenny bits. Our dismay was all in the mind, for we had nothing to spend the money on, mainly because we never went into a shop or, for that matter, any other commercial outlet.

In the evening there was Compline. Even at that young age, I felt the beauty of this contemplative office. In particular, I recall readings from Psalm 91, pregnant with symbolism: *Thou shalt not be afraid for the terror by night; nor the arrow that flieth by day; nor for the pestilence that walketh in darkness; nor for the destruction that wasteth at noonday. A thousand shall fall at thy side, and ten thousand at thy right hand; but it shall not come nigh thee."* I suppose now that the experience was part aesthetic, part emotional and part spiritual, and it is illuminating to contemplate the similarity of such encounters fifty-five years later. When almost every other aspect of life has changed, many beyond recognition, it is quite chilling now to make connections between these deeply affective processes.

Our other service was Benediction, with the singing of 'O Salutaris Hostia', 'Tantum Ergo' and 'Adoremus'. I can still feel the thrill of the ceremony when it was my turn to lead the singing. Although

Mass in the School Chapel

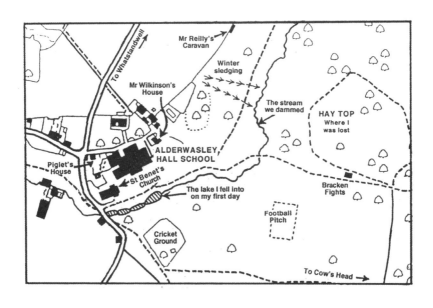

Alderwasley Hall Prep School and surrounding area

the Head had told my parents that my treble voice was good enough for Westminster Cathedral Choir, it was not until I was ten that I was allowed to undertake this responsibility, principally on account of my errant behaviour. Despite the fact that his worries were, in my view, unfounded, I have not forgotten the agony of failing to remember the tune of the 'Adoremus' right up to about ten seconds before I was due to start the singing. That it came to me at the very last moment could only have been, in my view at the time, an example of divine inspiration.

FUN, FUN, FUN

The countryside surrounding Alderwasley Hall was quite stunning and, even at that young, age I think we appreciated its space and beauty. Away across the Derwent gorge we could see the lighthouse at Crich Cliff, but in between there were wooded hills, brackened slopes and pasture with grazing cows. A stream ran across the fields at the bottom of the main hill on which the school stood, and one of our favourite activities was making dams with boulders, clods of red earth and terra cotta pipes to produce water spouts. The local farmer had given permission for this, just as long as the dams were taken down immediately at the end of our sessions. We worked on these feats of hydro-engineering like beings possessed, with each dam being designed and constructed by a team of about six boys, and each team anxious to outshine its rivals with innovatory ideas and scale of operation. I remember thinking that, if I were ever to be given a free choice, stream damming would be my future career.

Of comparable fulfilment were the occasional bracken fights. The secret of their success was determined by Mr Wilkinson and Mr Reilly who each organised a team and offered coaching on strategy and tactics. Usually, one side would attack a ruined Bothy in Alderwasley Park, whilst the other defended it. Our weapons were bracken stalks, stripped of their leaves and carried, roots uppermost, in our snake belts. When an enemy was identified, a boy would draw a weapon from his belt, rather in the manner of drawing a sword, hold it by the lighter end, and throw it spinning through the air at its target, just like a knife thrower. I still wonder how we did not all end up permanently scarred from these conflicts, for we developed high skill in hitting the enemy, even from some distance away. The only rule was one forbidding the hitting of somebody at very close range.

Not surprisingly, sport was an important feature of our week. On four afternoons a week we went on walks, but on the other three we had games, football in the winter and cricket in the summer. The main incentive as we grew older was to represent the School and, although my

46

interest in, and prowess at, cricket was quite modest, I did aspire to turning out for the football team. My first problem was that, whilst I had highly developed dribbling skills, my ability to shoot or clear the ball from defence was pretty awful. Thus, I was more likely to be brought on as a substitute in the second half, should someone be injured, than to start the game. The second difficulty lay in my inability to see football as a team game. My motivation was to mesmerise the opposition with spellbinding, defence-splitting solo runs, with no thought of passing to my team mates. Should I score, all would be forgiven, but if I were to squander possession on the altar of extravagance, I would attract the disapproval of teachers and boys alike. As a result, I made only occasional appearances at St Anselm's in Bakewell, Mickleover in Derby, or one of our other fixtures, although, as first reserve, I acquired much experience running the line.

We went on walks four afternoons a week. The main ones were the Packhorse Round, the Bear Inn Round and the New Round, but sometimes we took the opposite route to Shining Cliff Woods. The shortest of these was to Cow's Head, named after the shape of an old tree stump in the woods, and this was always the first walk that new boys went on. The longer walk was over Hay Top, a thickly-wooded hill where I once got lost. That experience was as frightening as any I can remember during my childhood years, for although I could hear Mr Wilkinson and some of the boys calling my name, I seemed to be moving further and further from them in my attempt to get out of the woods. As their voices became more distant, I faced with horror the prospect of never being rescued from what felt like an endless forest and, as darkness slowly began to fall, my desperation turned to despair. Eventually, I was found, and my relief was paralleled only by the teacher's. Never again did I leave the safety of the group on those woodland walks.

Very occasionally we walked into civilisation, where we actually encountered real people. One of these was a visit down to the river valley to the wire works about four miles from the school. I don't recall it being particularly educational, but it did represent a change from walking through forests and dry stone walls. We saw large coils of wire being moved from the manufacturing to the storage area, but we saw little of the actual wire-making process. The most exciting feature appeared just as we were about to leave. As the party set off on the return walk, my attention was attracted to a large cement mixer, noisily churning its load. As it was unattended, I decided to see what would happen if I turned the big metal wheel on the side of the mixer. There are times when you just have to do something, and this was one. Not surprisingly, the entire contents were deposited onto the ground in a grey, slippery heap. At that moment, a large, angry man - looking like Hardy from Laurel & Hardy - came out of a doorway and caught me in the act of sabotage. I looked along the track for moral support, but my group had turned the corner and were out of sight. All I could do was apologise and agree with everything the man said. At the least, no-one else at Alderwasley knew of my vandalism.

A much more light-hearted escapade was when Mr Wilkinson's alsatian, Sally, gave birth to eight pups who, when they were old enough, joined us on our walks. At any given moment, eight of us each had a twenty-minute session with a hyperactive pup on a lead, and this gave us all the pleasure of owning a pet with none of the attendant responsibilities. There were other animals around, most notably cows and the odd retired horse, as well as the multitude of rooks by whose croaking we were wakened each morning. When you add to this the conker fights, the building of dens, and the facility to wrestle at least three times a day, it is clear we were in schoolboy heaven, and I guess we knew it.

19491949194919491949194919491949199491949

FULL EXPOSURE

I am still not quite sure why I was caned so frequently, but I was and, at one point, I held the record for being caned on more occasions in a term than anyone else. It was a bitter-sweet experience, for although the pain was considerable, the notoriety, credibility and popularity that ensued made it more than worthwhile. We seemed to be caned for the most minor offences, like talking in Prep. I remember getting six for inappropriate behaviour in one of Mr James' History lessons. He had been talking to us about the Domesday Book and, when we were invited to ask questions, I asked if anyone knew the owner of the handkerchief lying on the floor by my desk. Oddly enough, I don't recall that we were ever struck by the injustice of such punishments at the time. We just accepted it as normal that sometimes you were caned for a misdemeanour perpetrated by someone else and, on other occasions, they might take the blame for you. I suppose the distribution was more or less equal over the length of a term.

Most punishments were for run-of-the-mill schoolboy mischief. Very rarely was there a really grievous misdemeanour, but there was a strong rumour that, if ever a really serious transgression was discovered - really bad swearing, blasphemy or lewd jokes - Billingham, the Head Boy, would report the incident to the Head in Latin rather than English, so as to embarrass neither of them, or so the story went. We were all most intrigued by this, and wished we had the courage to ask Billingham if he knew the Latin for 'knickers' or 'bottom' or 'breast' or 'willy' and other similarly rude words. We imagined that one of the prerequisites of being Head Boy was the compulsory learning of disgusting Latin words, which made this exalted position all the more desirable.

Quite the most daring school escapade I can recall was not one of my own, but was the result of a bet between two boys, Rudolph and Anthony. Rudolph was a strange boy, even by boarding school standards, where the most diverse and bizarre examples of pre-pubescent males seemed to congregate. He possessed a waterfall fringe of straight dark brown hair with a few strands standing vertically at the crown, heavy brows above scowling eyes, a protruding lower jaw and rounded shoulders, all of which combined to produce an anthropoid appearance, which was both amusing and disturbing. He wore longer grey shorts than the rest of us and had a habit of scratching the back of his right ear with five or six rapid flicks of his hand, rather in the manner of a flea-ridden dog. Above all, he was the archetypal conspirator who made bombs for others to throw. They, not he, took the consequences. Although I did not know it at the time, this was my first experience of schadenfreude.

Anthony, the elder of two brothers at the school, was much more of a conventional schoolboy, somewhat like Just William in personality and Bugs Bunny in appearance. He displayed a cheerful countenance with a sense of daring that occasionally landed him in trouble, but never more than on this particular occasion. He was always willing to take a bet, and the calculating Rudolph had presented him with a challenge that was both daunting and irresistible. Anthony's naive appetite for the dare, and the kudos it would afford him, was part of Rudolph's strategy. This was clearly a challenge that Anthony could not possibly refuse, and one that the rest of us could not resist.

Rudolph's bet was that Anthony would not be prepared to play the violin on his willy with a pen during a History lesson. The two ten-year olds stared at each other for about a minute, Rudolph inscrutable and Anthony hyperactively excited, until the latter reached across to shake hands with his comrade, thus accepting the wager. A handshake was a gesture of honour and could not be retracted. So it was that Mr James, blissfully unaware of these undercurrents, started the History lesson with the two boys on the front row, an indication of their low marks in last term's exams. That the lesson was delivered by the Headmaster just heightened the tension, and the anxiety was all the worse for those of us whose relatively strong academic performance in the previous term's examinations had denied us a close enough view of the action before us.

Nobody was remotely interested in the issues at stake in the Wars of the Roses on that warm summer morning. Precisely when Anthony would make his move was of much greater significance than what Henry Tudor was planning to do at Bosworth. The climax came after only five minutes of the lesson. By chance, the Headmaster asked an unexpected question about one of the battles and turned to Anthony for an answer. The boy was unaware that the spotlight had fallen upon him, for he was in the process of winning his bet and was looking triumphantly up from his groin towards Rudolph. The Head peered over the front of his desk to discover what had diverted Anthony's attention from the lesson and, in doing so, discovered the horrible truth of the erotic incident. Our corporate intake of breath was deafening.

Mr James had cultivated a practised air of angry disapproval, and we had all encountered it on occasions, but this time his demeanour was darker than we had ever before witnessed. Anthony was ordered to his dormitory with an operatic gesture, and we were set a passage to read whilst the forthcoming retribution got underway. Rudolph, never slow to exploit a good opportunity, took bets on how many strokes of the cane Anthony would receive for his transgression, partly to recoup his losses from the previous unsuccessful wager. In fact, we were all too shocked to gamble anything on the outcome, and some of the more impressionable members of the form wondered whether Anthony could survive the weight of punishment without serious injury.

By tradition, we always visited punished criminals in their dormitories after the Head had completed the operation and left. Thus, when break arrived, we rushed up to St Mark's to learn the true circumstances. This was indeed Anthony's greatest moment, largely overshadowing the pain of his punishment. He proceeded to tell us that 'Jammy' had given him no less sixteen strokes, and that these had landed randomly on various parts of his anatomy. We were intrigued and hungry for detail, and we knew from personal experience how erratic was the Headmaster's aim. Anthony, sublimating his obvious pain, milked the situation for all his worth, and there is no doubt that he was fully entitled to do so. "Well, the first one landed about here in the middle of my back...."

MOVING ON

The plan for my future education involved staying at Alderwasley until I was thirteen, at which point I would take the Common Entrance Examination and proceed to one of the major Catholic Public Schools - Douai, Downside, Ampleforth, Stonyhurst or Belmont. This was affordable on the strength of my Great Aunt Lucy's willingness to pay the fees. What it did not allow for was my father's coronary thrombosis late in 1948. It was not certain whether he would be able to complete his full teaching career and, within that uncertainty, a decision was made to bring me home at the end of the academic year and to find secondary education locally. So it was that, in the Spring of that year, I sat an examination that I had never before heard of, the Eleven Plus. Passing this would offer me a place either at St Mary's College, Crosby, a Catholic Grammar School run by the Irish Christian Brothers, or King George V School, a maintained Southport Grammar School with a high academic reputation. Because my mother had heard lurid tales about boys at St Mary's being beaten for almost any misdemeanour, the Crosby option was duly crossed off the list. (By coincidence, my first teaching appointment in 1960 was at a school run by that same religious order). If I passed, then, it was to be KGV.

When, at the age of eight, you have learned the meaning of metaphor, simile, alliteration, hyperbole and other parts of speech, and when, only three years later, you are confronting Latin gerundives and Pythagoras' Theorem, the facing of the Eleven Plus poses few problems. It might appear churlish to regret passing this examination with ease, but there really was a sting in the tale. The top thirty boys were placed in a Trans form, where their academic route was expressed by taking both O Level and A Level one year before everyone else. In years to come there would be a price to pay for this; one I shall reveal later. However, in the Summer of 1949 I was thrilled by the news that I had passed for King George V School and that I would soon be wearing the distinctive maroon and black blazer.

In the spring of 1949 my brother Denis married his fiancée, Joyce - known to everyone as Jay. She came from Woking in Surrey and was from a family of five children, her father being a professional photographer. Jay and Denis had met during the war when working together in the RAF base at Stoke Holy Cross near Norwich. In the late 1940s times were hard, and so they lived for two months in a rented house in Parbold before moving in with their friends in Shaws Road, Gwen and Tom Ball, until they could afford to buy a house of their own in Carr Lane. However, before that, their daughter, Susan, my niece and godchild, was born in 1950.

After leaving Prep School, I retained contact with only two of my schoolboy friends. Brian Ibberson, with whose family I had stayed in Matlock made two visits to Southport in subsequent years, but I finally lost touch with him when he emigrated to Australia. I met Tony Campbell in Wigan, now running his father's chemist's shop, after discovering that his mother was on the Governing Body of the Grammar

School to which I was appointed on entering the teaching profession in 1960. As for the others, I really know very little. I remember reading that Mark Honoré had attained high status in British Leyland, and I recently discovered that Andrzej Morawicz is now the President of the Federation of Poles in Great Britain. I was also told that Morris was in jail, and that reminded me of the day we were waiting in the yard for a walk to commence when a rook dropped its load of excrement from a great height, smack onto his head. With his dark brown basin haircut topped with slimy white, he resembled a large Christmas pudding.

Returning home in summer 1949 gave me the chance to sample some of the foods that had disappeared during the war. I had frequently seen pictures of monkeys eating bananas in my comics, and I was keen to try one as soon as they returned to the shops. As often happens when levels of anticipation are high, the reality was most disappointing, for I had expected bananas to be juicy, not dry. Wall's vanilla ice cream was also something of a let-down as it was available as a 'Wall's Brick', most aptly named. On the other hand, Maltesers greatly exceeded my expectations, and the same applied to Crunchie bars which, in those days, had two layers of chocolate coating, one milk and one plain. With the addition of Dandelion & Burdock pop, Pontefract Cakes, Uncle Joe's Mint Balls, as well as chips from Barton's on the way to Silcock's Fair on the field at Isle of Wight Farm at the bottom of Guildford Road, my schoolboy diet underwent a huge and wonderful transformation.

In so many ways I was to miss boarding school. Aside from my two serious emotional crises - being caned on the first night and returning to school four days earlier than was necessary - life had been almost uninterrupted joy. The mixture of hard academic work, a structured routine, a setting within which to develop independence, a gorgeous natural environment, and the stimulating and competitive company of boys of similar age, all combined to provide an ideal agent for learning and growing up. The only missing piece of the jigsaw was the ability to be with one's parents on a daily basis.

At Alderwasley Hall, I had assimilated some of the principles of co-existence, of giving as well as taking, and of accepting that injustice has sometimes to be endured without protest or resentment. I had also learned not to cry, at least not in public. I treasure those experiences learned in the late-1940s, and I have no doubt that foundations laid during that time provided me with the means of coping successfully with some of life's subsequent problems, adventures and responsibilities. Of course, those of us who are lucky enough to be optimists probably tend to focus upon and recall the good things at the expense of unhappier times. Well, so be it.

PART THREE
ON TO GRAMMAR SCHOOL
1949-55

NEW BOYS TOGETHER
MUSICAL HIGHS AND LOWS
LET'S BOO SILVERTON
PILOT OF THE FUTURE
WHEN I LAST SAW MY FATHER
GOING AWAY
FIRST WHEELS; FIRST KISS
PLAYING FOR SPENCER'S
SHALL WE DANCE?
THE WORLD OF WORK
WAITING FOR A SOUTHPORT BUS
BEING IN THE SIXTH FORM
I WISH I'D SAID THAT TO HIM
NEW DOORS OPENING

1949194919491949194919491949194919491949

NEW BOYS TOGETHER

There was a full school assembly on our first morning at King George V School. To all of us new boys it was a grand and awesome ceremony and, at the end, we were asked to remain in our seats after everyone else had left. The Headmaster was Geoffrey Dixon. Although we did not know it at the time, he also was new to the school, having been appointed Head at the age of thirty-six, unusually young to lead a staff whose average age must have been over fifty. Wearing academic robes and with a dignified and strict bearing, he read out our names, pausing at the end of each form list, at which point we filed out behind whoever was our form master. I was in Trans X, made up of boys whose performance in the 11+ exam had identified them as academic high-fliers and, as such, destined to sit the O level and A level exams one year ahead of others in their age group.

The seating arrangement in our form room was alphabetical and, looking towards the blackboard, I sat on the right-hand row, third from the front. This order was also replicated in the register, listing Ashurst, Ashworth, Bagshaw, Ball, Booth, Bowman, Bradford, Croston and so on up to Wright, who moved down to 2A at the end of the year. There were few changes in the composition of the form, but some promotions and demotions occurred between the Trans and the A form, and very occasionally with the

53

B form. There was a plan for boys at secondary modern schools to gain grammar school places through the 12-plus and 13-plus examinations, but this was largely frustrated by the fact that most grammar schools had hardly any spare places. In general, the chances of most boys and girls finding places in grammar schools was determined largely by where they lived. In some parts of the country 25% of the age group might pass the eleven plus; in others it might only be 12%, and this was governed strictly by the number of places available.

The form master of Trans X was Hubert Evans. Since we had three Evans on the staff, he was known as 'Little Taff', and we liked him immensely. He was a friendly man, short and portly with white hair and black-rimmed glasses. He spoke with a mild Welsh lilt and was an ideal person to help new boys settle in. Above all, he was a first-class teacher, challenging our intellects, involving every boy in the lesson and offering frequent praise whenever appropriate. He taught us English, French and Latin and we learned enthusiastically. I recall vividly our French textbook by Whitmarsh. It featured two French children, Marcel and Denise, who involved themselves in a series of experiences in order to teach us the language in an interesting way, mainly by means of line drawings accompanied by a choice of written descriptions from which we had to choose the correct one. Over the year Marcel and Denise acted out dozens of little dramas for our benefit and, although there was no evidence of sexual chemistry between them, this proved a relatively painless means of learning a foreign language.

One of the idiosyncratic features of these lessons was the method used by Mr Evans to award marks, both for tests and for homeworks. For twenty correct answers we gained twenty marks, plus a bonus of two for getting then all right, with a further allowance of up to five for presentation. Thus, the top mark available was 20 + 2 + 5, which was a pleasure to announce when we called out our marks by alphabetical form order as he wrote them into his register. Latin was also taught partly by means of pictures in that first year. The very first line in our black text book, 'Latin for Today', instructed us to look at the illustration: "Discipuli Picturam Spectate".

Along with two other boys I had a particular problem with much of the work in Trans X because I had learned it already at my prep school. In our first exams I was top in Maths, second in Latin and third in French, and the other two performed similarly well. On this basis, we were probably identified as future State Scholars and Oxbridge certainties, but the chances of attaining either of these prizes was denied me as a result of several factors, one of which was my own appalling lack of judgement. As time went by the others in the form were catching up to our level and, when

The handsome frontage of King George V School

Group photograph with the author on the right of the middle row

we moved into Trans Y at the beginning of the second year, we were only a few months ahead of our form mates. At this point the two others who shared this advantage started to work harder, but I languished in my self-indulgent state of inertia, assuming that success would continue without further sacrifice. This, alongside the death of my father shortly after my thirteenth birthday, produced the bizarre outcome of a boy who was top of his age group in Maths during his first year taking three attempts before passing the subject at O level three years later.

KGV had a house system and, on arrival, we were placed in one of the eight houses, each named after a former member of staff. I was in Spencer's and my housemaster was Mr Marsden. He was known to my father and that was why I had been placed under his care. Bill Marsden, a distinguished historian, was small and round, which explained his nickname of 'Fat Bill'. He spoke in a characteristic Lancashire accent with a strong rolling 'r', indicative of a Preston background. The house meetings took place in classrooms enlarged by the folding back of wooden screens to increase the space available, and this extra square footage was occupied by Mr Marsden and the house prefects who sat facing the rest of us. Our house captain was J.C.Higgins, and the fact that he was also Captain of School gave us all additional Spencerian pride. The remaining sixty of us crammed into the desks in twos for these assemblies.

One of the significant benefits of the house system was the providing of a communication system between the younger and the older boys. If I wished I could speak to Higgins and others of his age without embarrassment, and he could respond in a kindly, paternal way. The other feature of the system was that it provided a cause to fight in competition with the other seven, whether at Rugby or Cricket or Athletics or anything else. Most of all, it afforded us the opportunity to go crazy for one word of the School Song, once a term. As the chorus began, "Mason's, Grear's and the rest of them; their names shall live for aye," we all substituted "Spencer's" or whatever house we were in, shouting at the tops of our voices in a full end-of-term assembly. The chorus ended "King George the Fifth School once again shall make the rafters ring". Three times a year, and for just one word, we did.

1950195019501950195019501950195019501950

MUSICAL HIGHS AND LOWS

King George V School - KGV as it was and is still known - was renowned for its musical performances, and so I joined the choir soon after starting. Although the content of the music lessons was not too exciting - 'Drink to me only', in particular - some of the works we sang for the annual

56

music concert were varied and stimulating. Although I had sung at Mass, Compline and Benediction whilst at Alderwasley, the mode had been plainsong or unison singing, with the occasional descant, and so this was my first introduction to part singing in general, and to four-part singing in particular. Our music teacher was Ken Eglin, a man of wit and personality who enthused us to perform to the limits of our capabilities. We liked him because, although our routine music was rather conventional, he would sometimes play jazz for us. Our commitment to the choir practices was, therefore, driven largely by our respect for him and, as someone who was later to enter the profession, I am aware that teaching ability generally outshines lesson content as a means of inspiring children of all ages.

We rehearsed and rehearsed for month after month. Some practices were for younger boys, the trebles and altos, whilst others were for the full choir with the tenors and basses joining us. The orchestra, in which I was to make a brief but unrepeated appearance, practised separately. The final rehearsal in front of the School was a stomach-churning experience - the mixture of anxiety and enjoyment that makes performing so wonderful and affecting. The night itself, in March 1950, was on an even higher plane. Large vases of flowers lined the front of the stage and the first two rows of the audience were occupied by prestigious dignitaries in their full regalia. We were all packed together on a large tiered platform with unbroken voices at the front and older boys at the back, all in all about sixty of us. I stood next to Blundell, who sang just like a starving seagull, and tried hard not to listen to him. The curtains opened to reveal row after row of kindly adult faces who had all paid one shilling (5p) for the privilege of listening to us. Mr Eglin, in dinner jacket and black bow-tie, presided over the performance, whilst the orchestra was augmented by two members of staff, Mr Flemming on flute and Mr Booth on timpani. In years to come, four or five musicians from the Southport High School for Girls would join our orchestra and we liked this because it gave us something interesting to look at when we weren't singing.

My parents were in the audience and I was later told that my mother cried when we sang 'Linden Lea' by Vaughan Williams. The orchestra of twenty-six players bravely tackled a number of pieces, including works by Schubert, Purcell and Haydn, but the most inspiring passages for me were when choir and orchestra combined to produce strong renditions of 'The Hundredth Psalm', 'Jerusalem' and Zion's Children'. These are the great performance moments - the tingling scalp, the moist eyes. And then...it is over. I came into school the following morning with a sensation close to that of bereavement. For months we had worked on our choir pieces, improving pitch and developing phrasing, but today there was nothing. We had been compulsorily retired. All that rehearsing and, in particular, the camaraderie that accompanied it had reached its climax in under two hours and was now in the past. Nevertheless, its faint after-image was reflected in the shy smiles we choir members gave each other, irrespective of age, as we passed in the corridors. We retained the exultation of a shared experience and we felt what is nowadays referred to as 'corporate pride'.

I remained in the choir throughout my time at KGV, moving to the tenors when, after an interminably embarrassing delay, my voice finally broke. A small number of the most dedicated of us also joined the madrigal choir where the singing of Elizabethan music recreated some of the pleasure I had enjoyed in Compline at Alderwasley five years earlier. In the main choir we sang many inspiring pieces, but few were as fulfilling as the extracts we performed from Haydn's Creation, and the emotion of 'In Native Worth' as well as the dynamism of 'The Heavens are Telling' remain with me. The orchestra's quality improved and our headmaster, Geoffrey Dixon, became the regular leading cellist. Ken Eglin left and was replaced by a dedicated but shy music teacher called Mr Williams. He had a nervous twitch that gave him an immediate nickname, yet the older boys warmed to his sense of commitment and did not make fun of him as the younger ones did. I imagine that we felt protective towards him.

Our two greatest achievements, in my view, were the renderings of Handel's 'Zadok the Priest' and the Polovtsian Dances from 'Prince Igor' by Borodin, although I should mention that we sang it rather than danced it. The tenor part was excruciatingly high, and it would certainly have been easier for me to reach the notes before, rather than after, my voice had broken. Fortunately, this piece was the finale in the concert, which was just as well because I do not think we possessed the ability to continue afterwards. Whenever I hear the piece today I am transported back to a time when there was very little in life that surpassed the sheer joy of making music together.

By the age of twelve I had been playing the piano for about nine years, and so what prompted me to change to the violin I will never know. I can only guess that I thought this move would increase my chance of participating in the school orchestra, which it did, but very much on a one-off basis. I bought my violin, complete with case, bow and resin, from Miss Mungall who lived in Dunkirk Road. She was a pleasant Scotswoman, but she had an obsessive determination that I should hold the violin only by pressure from my chin and not held in any way by my fingering hand. Each lesson I would start in the correct way but, as time passed, the violin was supported increasingly lazily by my left hand. As soon as Miss Mungall spotted this, she would snatch the instrument away from my chin with a knowing chuckle and say, "Now look, Paul, you are not holding that violin properly...again!" After being caught out routinely, the day came when I resolved to hold the violin rest with my chin in a vice-like grip. As a mater of habit, Miss Mungall pulled the instrument from what she assumed was a feeble hold and, as her irresistible force met my immovable object, we very nearly ended up in a heap on the floor.

I reflected that the young Menuhin would never have suffered this kind of indignity, and I had received the first of several indications that I was not born to be a violinist. Practising was an excruciating experience, both for me and for my family, and the call of football on Bedford Park with Peter Croston, David Gott, Nen and 'Lucy' Smith became ever stronger. I did make one appearance with the school orchestra, and I did play with great confidence in that part of a Scarlatti divertimento that has an open string D for the second violins for sixteen bars. Sadly, this was the summit of my own musical development and, two years after taking up this impossible instrument, I sold it back to Miss Mungall for exactly what I had paid for it, twenty-six shillings (£1.30). I did not see tears in her eyes as the transition was made but, in fairness, she had done the best she could with me. My great mistake, of course, was in not returning to the piano.

LET'S BOO SILVERTON

No matter how interesting lessons may have been, the time of the day we looked forward to with the greatest enthusiasm was lunch-time, known in the north of England as 'dinner time'. It has to be said that the attraction was not eating but the playing of football. We were issued with 'form balls' and so Trans X, like all the other forms, had a ball at its disposal for the entire mid-day break. The only problem was that we were given Rugby balls and we wanted to play soccer, despite the strong tradition of the 15-a-side game at KGV. In fact, we turned this difficulty to our advantage, for we all developed the rarified skill of controlling the oval ball with our feet, a craft which takes considerable practice to develop. Any master who had to teach us first lesson in the afternoon was faced with thirty tousle-haired, sweaty-faced, dirty-kneed boys whose presence in his lesson was more than slightly begrudging.

A small number of boys would do other things during the lunch break. Some would use the library, particularly on very wet days, whilst others would meet with friends in the Bee Club or other societies. For most of us, nothing could possibly compete with football even in the most awful weather, that is, until the time of the Mock Election. This event in 1950 was a new sport, albeit a spectator one, and it did not resemble anything we had experienced before. Four members of the Sixth Form were candidates: Wynne - Conservative, Wignall - Labour, Levin - Liberal, and Silverton -

Communist. These hardy individuals braved the raucous heckling of the schoolboy electorate in order to explain their policies and capture our votes. Three of the candidates managed to make themselves heard for at least some of the time, and there were isolated occasions when boys would listen to political arguments and ask intelligent questions. Not so with Silverton who, for reasons known only to himself, had nailed his flag to the Communist mast, perhaps for sheer devilment. A great adventure for the younger boys was to follow him around the school grounds and, with a level of impunity never before enjoyed, boo a member of the Sixth Form.

We all imagined that we understood a little about politics, mainly because we had heard it discussed by our parents and, very occasionally, had listened to Party Political Broadcasts on the radio. We thought we knew what the main parties stood for, although I don't suppose we did, but when it came to Communism we were confronted with a completely unencountered species. We might not have known what a Communist was, but we did know that you booed them, and so the lunch break now presented us with a new and difficult choice. "What shall we do? Shall we play football...or shall we boo Silverton?" For most of the time until the election was over we said, "Er...let's boo Silverton".

PILOT OF THE FUTURE

Comics in my day were of some interest, but I cannot recall any burning enthusiasm for them until, on 14th April 1950, the Eagle was born. Up to that point I had worked my way through Chicks Own, Tiny Tots, the Dandy and the Beano, as well as Rupert Bear and Babar the Elephant. Older boys read Rover, Hotspur and Wizard, as well as an assortment of American comics, but I was never drawn to them. The Eagle, which called itself a magazine rather than a comic, was inspired by the Reverend Marcus Morris, Vicar of St James Church, Birkdale, who received support from the Reverend Chad Varah, the founder of the Samaritans. Frank Hampson, the chief illustrator, had studied at Southport School of Art and Craft in the late 1940s, and his style was notably more innovatory and polished than most of the others in the field. Because of this, and the vision of Marcus Morris, this new publication represented a major advance within its genre and, at one stage, Arthur C Clarke was adviser to the scriptwriting team. Parents who had previously frowned upon the content of most comics were pleased to welcome higher quality reading for their children, and so the Eagle enjoyed greater acceptability than any of its predecessors.

The first few editions were lighter in colour than the rest because there was apparently some technical difficulty with the advanced photogravure printing process that they had chosen to ensure high quality.

Apparently, the watercolour originals were not as strong as required and, for this reason, reds were pink, yellows were cream and all other colours were correspondingly paler than intended, but the strength and style of Hampson's fluent line-drawings held the designs together successfully. Within a short period, inks were used instead of watercolour in order to address the problem. Unlike other comics, where the pictures were produced in a story-board style of identical squares, the Eagle sometimes divided its pages into a variety of shapes - circles, triangles, parallelograms, and so on. The team of artists worked from an improvised studio in a former bakery cookhouse on Botanic Road, Churchtown, at the northern end of Southport.

The main character in the Eagle was Dan Dare, Pilot of the Future, and the stories were set in 1995. He was a rakishly handsome officer with a large chin and eccentrically angular eyebrows, and he wore the green uniform and cap of a Colonel in the Interplanet Spacefleet, an arm of the United Nations World Government. Dan's boss was Sir Hubert Guest, the Controller of the Interplanet Spacefleet, based loosely upon Woodvale Aerodrome to the south of Southport. Dan's batman was called Digby, whilst his leading female character was Professor Peabody, a constant thorn in Sir Hubert's side. Her character was based upon one of the team of artists, Greta Tomlinson, whilst Sir Hubert was modelled on Frank Hampson's father, Robert, and several of the other personalities, including Tommy Walls - the Boy Wonder, resembled Southport people of the early 1950s. The Eagle was printed by Eric Bemrose of Liverpool and published by the Hulton Press, whose titles at the time included Picture Post and Lilliput. It was immediately recognisable because it was larger than its competitors, was printed largely in colour, and was, quite simply, the best. Although the cost of threepence was a penny more than other comics in 1950, it enjoyed an average circulation of over two million copies.

Dan Dare's ingenuity and courage were tested to the full by his main enemies, the Treens, who came from Venus. They were green with angular features and wide mouths, and they wore a flexible golden armour, something like a broad shower hose. The Mekon, their leader, had an enormous head, presumably to contain his massive brain, and he spent most of his time floating in a cross-legged position. Sondar, the friendly Treen, leaked secrets like mad to Dan and his associates, and it is a wonder that he was never suspected of being a double agent, in view of the Mekon's huge intellect. Populating the other end of Venus were the Therons, with blue skin, blond hair and Roman soldier-style skirts. They had a power-bulge on their foreheads, which spoiled an otherwise elegant appearance. When Col. Dan Dare and the Interplanet Spacefleet were locked in heavy conflict with those Treens, the Therons were the late arrivals on Dan's side

Bronze bust of Dan Dare

My father with his books

Sister-in-law Jay with daughter Susan

rather like the Americans in two world wars and Blucher at Waterloo. There were other adventures, such as that when Hank and Pierre, two of Dan's colleagues, ran out of fuel in the asteroid belt, but they were fortunately rescued after a fading radio signal was picked up by Digby.

The Eagle contained quite a number of strip cartoons in addition to the main story. There was Harris Tweed, a rather bumbling detective with a boy helper, Tommy Walls, the Boy Wonder, who made a W-sign with his fingers - a risky gesture today perhaps - whenever he needed to fly. He was something of a junior superman, dressed in the corporate colours of Walls Ice Cream, with yellow shirt and blue shorts, wisely avoiding the cape, mask and red underwear of the real thing. PC 49 of radio fame appeared at some point, as did Riders of the Range. One of the most spectacular sections was where Professor Brittain explained how things worked, often accompanied by large, highly-detailed sectional views of ocean liners or express steam locomotives.

The front of the comic had a red square with "Eagle - Every Friday' printed in golden yellow, along with a stylised picture of the bird of prey. It was unashamedly male in style, but a sister comic - 'Girl' - appeared a little later. It is sad to record that the Eagle was eventually taken over and suffered something of a drop in quality, but nothing can erase the memory of the excitement it provided for boys across the country in the 1950s...every Friday.

195119511951195119511951195119511951

WHEN I LAST SAW MY FATHER

Mr father's first heart attack precipitated my leaving of prep school, the sitting and passing of the eleven plus examination and the subsequent entry into King George V School. Almost exactly two years later, towards the end of 1950, he had a second coronary thrombosis and this was the one from which he would not recover. He was fifty-seven but, in many ways, physically much older. He had been a heavy smoker and had suffered from yellow fever during the first world war. He took no exercise and all of his hobbies, interests and occupations were sedentary in nature. He went into hospital in December, returning home for Christmas. The bed was moved into the lounge for my father's comfort, and a lasting image I retain is of him holding Susan, my niece and godchild, in his arms. She was then about 18 months old and was a sheer delight to him. A grand-daughter must have been, in some way, compensation for the wife and the daughter he had lost, and she would be a member of Farnborough Road School, just as he and I had been. He would not live to see her second birthday.

My father was readmitted to hospital in the following February before dying on the thirteenth day. On that day my mother visited him at the Liverpool Royal Infirmary. I was unaware of the seriousness of his condition, but I sensed that something was wrong when she returned home late in the afternoon. "Your daddy is very ill," she told me. It was only when my Uncle Lou arrived from Warrington and put his arm around me that the full truth was exposed, and I can remember sobbing for the rest of the evening. Later I had irrational thoughts, ranging from imagining that the hospital had made a mistake and that he was still alive, to the notion that yesterday had been a dream and that my father would still be with us when I wakened. Perhaps we realise the depth of our love only when its object is no longer there. The emotions are several, but guilt is inevitably one of them. Had my behaviour exacerbated his condition? Would he have lived longer had I shown more consideration? Why wasn't my mother crying? I had not yet perceived that her stoicism was for the protection of my feelings and that she was weeping alone.

My father died intestate, and so my mother's other concern was financial. When his affairs were finally settled there was not a lot of money, because he was never a saver. She did not even receive a widow's pension, for my father had not sufficient stamps on his card. My brother and sister-in-law provided some support during this difficult time and, should a crisis have arisen, Auntie Lucy was there to help, but my mother now faced two courses of action. Firstly, she would have to sell my father's book collection. This was a heartbreaking process because, despite the abundance of valuable first editions he had accumulated over the years, her need to make a quick sale prevented the receiving of anywhere near their true value. The second course was to find a job. Her first paid occupation after my father's death was as a door-to-door collector for the Provident Clothing Company, whereby women bought stamps on a weekly basis and later cashed them in for articles of clothing, a forerunner of the mail-order catalogue. I imagine that this must have been the darkest point in her life, and that she was relieved when the opportunity came for her to work in the dress department of Boothroyd's on Lord Street, where she had more dignity and enjoyed the company of colleagues. She later worked in a similar capacity at Richard Shops, and this was necessary, not just for day to day living, but also to keep me in education for as long as was necessary - in fact, a further ten years.

Immediately after my father died, I was bought my first long trousers. This was, to some extent, a symbol of my being 'the man of the house', a rôle I did not feel at all ready to assume, but one at which I would have to do my best. I liked the grown-up status that long trousers conferred but, in every other way, I would have preferred shorts which, in the 1950s, were normal dress for boys up to the age of fourteen. For this reason I received the customary ridicule for 'wearing drainpipes' from my KGV form mates on my return to school after a period of absence, although I must concede that their taunts were combined with a kindness that boys do not routinely display to each other at that age. Another change was the receiving of free school dinners, for which my mother was entitled to apply. I assumed that I must be the only boy in the school who did not pay for his meals, and I was terrified that this secret would be revealed and that I would have to leave the school rather than suffer the consequent shame. I suppose I also believed that I was the only one at KGV without a father and that, because of this, I was somehow incomplete, rather as I now imagine a widow must feel.

GOING AWAY

After my father died my mother and I went away for weekends about twice a month. I imagine that she could not face the uninterrupted periods at home and that she also needed the company of relatives that these visits would bring. There were two locations: Auntie Mildred's in Chester Road, Warrington, and Auntie Mona's in Heaton Moor, Stockport. Mildred Tickle had a husband, Jimmy, and two boys, David who was four years younger than I, and Ian who was still a baby. Also living there was Will Hales, my maternal grandfather. It was a small house across the river from Thames Board where my Uncle Jimmy worked as a stores clerk. Mona lived in a three-bedroomed semi-detached house on the Manchester side of Stockport. Her husband, Edgar Howells, was a cost accountant at McVitie & Price Biscuits in Levenshulme, and my cousin John, attending William Hulme Grammar School, was 18 months younger than I was.

The visits to Warrington were less attractive to me because there was no-one of my age in the household. Although it was possible to travel to and from Warrington by train, the journey was complicated and involved travelling by the Cheshire Lines Railway from Lord Street Station. To simplify the operation, we went by bus and, at that age, I was a pathetic martyr to travel sickness. The worst of these journeys was on a bus owned by St Helens Corporation, draughted onto a route normally served by Ribble Buses. It had recently been repainted inside and out, and the combination of paint smell and jerky movement proved too much for my sensitive stomach to bear. To my great embarrassment, the driver was asked to stop the bus on three occasions during the two-hour journey so that I could vomit by the roadside. As we alighted at the Ritz Cinema to walk across the iron bridge to Chester Road, carrying our suitcases, my face was as white as a sheet and my head ached. Less than forty-eight hours later I would be forced to undergo a similar ordeal on the return journey.

Our route to Stockport was primarily by train from Chapel Street, Southport, to Manchester Victoria, although we did take an 89 or 92 bus from Manchester to Heaton Moor. I arrived in a much better physical state than after the Warrington run, and I did not dread the journey home, even though I should have wished the stay to have been longer. My mother took cakes and pies to both her sisters' houses as part of our contribution to the weekend stay. The main advantage for me at Stockport was that John was fairly close to me in age, and we were more like brothers, sharing the same interests and eccentric sense of humour. We played cricket and football, went train and bus spotting and built up a large collection of hand painted model buses.

It was this latter interest that prompted a most unusual happening. One day an accountant colleague of my Uncle Edgar came to visit him at Heaton Road. Before he left he looked into the front room to say hello to John and me. We were absorbed in our fleet of over fifty model buses, and he took a great interest in what we were doing, asking questions about our collection, picking up and admiring particular models, and generally being charming and friendly. After he left, my cousin looked at me suddenly with a shocked expression. "He's stolen one!" he announced, and ran into the next room to tell his father. Quite understandably he was just not believed initially. After all, grown-ups simply don't do that sort of thing. We were quite certain, for when you have hand painted, numbered and catalogued large fleets of individual models, you know at once when one is missing. John eventually persuaded his father that the impossible had happened, but we both realised that my uncle could not accuse his colleague of stealing, and we simply had to resign ourselves to accepting the loss.

One of our hobbies was the designing of surreal machines, such as a combined bus and steamroller that could transport passengers and roll the road at the same time. We were inspired by the whimsical humour of pedal power, and many hours were spent drawing pedal-driven helicopters, fighter planes, crop sprayers and even auto-change record players. Our main obsession was with table football, and we spent years organising teams, naming and painting players, arranging transfers and working through enormous seasons of league, cup and other competitions. At the peak, we each had about twenty-four teams, not to mention foreign touring sides who visited our leagues on a temporary basis. All of this was often at the expense of time that should have been spent on weekend homework. When my cousin's youngest daughter, Helena, was married in 2000, John and I played two games of table football, still with those original players from the 1950s, on the snooker table before leaving to attend the wedding.

66

John and I shared a passion for football and, in particular, for Manchester United. My own interest started in 1948 when they had beaten Blackpool 4-2 in the FA Cup Final, having been two goals down at half-time. I still remember the team: Crompton; Carey, Aston; Anderson, Chilton, Cockburn; Delaney, Morris, Rowley, Pearson, Mitten. Our visits to Old Trafford were few, but we did go to Edgeley Park to watch Stockport County on several occasions. The very worst of these was a goalless draw with Chester, and the match was so feeble that we walked to the top of the terraces and watched the trains instead of the football. Perhaps I had been spoiled because, after my father died, Wilf Gott, father of David and Thelma, was kind enough to take me with them to watch Everton at Goodison Park. He drove a big Rover 90 at great speed and, quite often, the journey was considerably more exciting than the game.

The only time the journey to Stockport caused a problem was when I decided to go by bike. Because it was warm when I set off from home, I wore my PE kit to keep cool. Unfortunately, the weather changed from sunshine to rain during my journey and I had to travel the length of the East Lancs Road amongst heavy lorries spraying my white vest, shorts and socks with black mud. I arrived at my aunt's house totally exhausted and looking like a Victorian boy chimney sweep, and I was put straight into the bath whilst my clothes were washed. The situation was not helped by the fact that I had not told my mother anything about the proposed venture, and she was not easy to pacify. As we did not have a telephone, the message had to be sent through a neighbour, and that did nothing to reduce her anger. Moreover, I had taken no extra clothes with me and, since nothing belonging to John or Uncle Edgar would fit me well enough to avoid absolute ridicule, I had to return home in my PE kit, drawing strange looks from passers by. Having been strictly forbidden from making the return journey by road, I took my bike on the bus with the kind cooperation of the conductor, and in the guard's van of the train from Victoria to Southport. My reception at home was distinctly cool.

As years passed, the need to escape from Lyndhurst Road at weekends was reduced, although regular contact with our relatives was maintained, and I remain in close communication with John Howells, wherever in the world he happens to be working. Of the previous generation, all have now died, the last being Auntie Mildred in 1999 at the age of ninety. As my godmother, she was just a bit special to me, particularly after the death of my mother, ten years earlier. As for the rest of us, we are still breathing at the time of writing.

In addition to the weekends away, my mother and I took annual summer holidays for a few years after my father died. She did her very best to find locations which would provide an interest for me, but there was no doubt that she was missing my father terribly or that I was lacking the company of those of my own age. It is upsetting to recall that, although we both must have been unfulfilled by these excursions, neither wanted to risk offending the other by appearing to have anything less than a good time. On the first occasion we went to Cleveleys and stayed at the Morvern Hotel on the sea front. Cleveleys was not very exciting, but you could go by tram into Blackpool where there was plenty to do, even though it was very expensive. The holiday was agreeable, if not action-packed, and I found enough to occupy myself for the eight days we were there.

One afternoon we were sitting on deck chairs on a warm beach when my mother suggested that I might like to swim, and so I returned to the hotel to change into my swimming trunks. I had just completed the change when there was a knock at the bedroom door. It was the hotel proprietor, Mr W, asking if he could come in and, with the typical naivety of a thirteen-year-old, I said yes. In truth, I couldn't think of a reason to refuse. He entered and sat on the edge of the bed. His manner was warm and intimate in a way that seemed to me inappropriate for someone I hardly knew, but I had no choice but to accept it. He said that he hoped I was enjoying my holiday, and assured me that I would always be welcome at his hotel. Then, Mr W alarmed me by admiring my swimming trunks and saying how well they suited me, at which point I started to experience a sinking feeling in my stomach. He asked me what material they were made from. I said I didn't know. Were they a comfortable fit? I nodded, swallowing hard. He then observed that the front of the trunks would probably be double-strength, and asked me if I knew why this would be. I shook my head and, at this latest question, began to panic. I mumbled something incoherent about my mother expecting me and that she would be wondering where I was, and then walked out of the bedroom, leaving him sitting on my bed. I was shaking as I walked out of the hotel and onto the beach.

For the remaining three days of our stay at the Morvern, Mr W was extremely charming and helpful to us both, anxious to please in any way he could. We got extra helpings without asking, and it was clear that he was buying my co-operation. Despite this, I could not help noticing that he avoided eye contact with me on every single occasion. Each time he came near us, I felt a sickening wave of embarrassment and revulsion. Just like so many innocent children who find themselves in similar circumstances, I never told my mother anything of the incident, either then or later, and this account is the very first time I have revealed it to anyone. It was my good fortune that, unlike so many poor young people who do not manage to escape in the way I did, the experience was the only one of its kind ever to confront me.

1952195219521952195219521952195219521952

FIRST WHEELS; FIRST KISS

Early in 1952 I very reluctantly sold my Hornby Dublo model railway, principally because I was afraid of being thought childish if I kept it. Soon after that, I got my first two-wheeler bike. It wasn't new, but that did not bother me because not many boys' families could afford new bikes in those days, mainly on account of the shortage of metal after the war. The problem was that it was a ladies' bike and no amount of re-painting, re-designing or customising would disguise that. To retain some sort of dignity I mounted the bicycle as though it had a cross-bar in the way that boys do and, at one point, I even considered making a cross-bar out of an old bicycle pump. The handlebars were sit-up-and-beg in style, but they had been mounted upside down to give the cycle a slightly more modern appearance. Although I was most grateful for this present, I always attempted to park it in the cycle sheds unseen.

Only about a year later I became the proud possessor of a men's bike with continental drop handlebars. Once again, it was not new, and it was painted entirely in black, but it did have a cross-bar as well as a three-speed Sturmy Archer gear change, so my street credibility improved considerably. I now started to ride to KGV behind the school bus, something that had been unthinkable as long as I rode a ladies' bike. Although buses are somewhat faster than bikes, I always caught up with the bus before it left the next stop, and this was important because girls from the High School occupied the downstairs section, and those who sat at the back on the six sideways seats could see me. What was more important was that I could see them, but I often adopted the appearance of not noticing them by failing to make eye contact in the hope that this action would give me a more enigmatic and faintly unattainable air. I also wore my cap on the back of my head to look even more windswept and stylish, but this was a risky action because, if the wind blew it off, all my cultivated nonchalance would be sacrificed by the need to go back and retrieve it, thus failing in my plan to keep up with the bus.

One morning I came to get on my bike to find that the back tyre was flat. I had no puncture repair kit and my pump was broken, so I had to walk up to Liverpool Road to get the school bus. I was not to know that this chance occurrence was to open up a new and delightful series of encounters. The tradition on the bus was for the KGV boys to go upstairs and for the High School girls to occupy the downstairs seats. When I got to the top of the bus there were no spare seats, and so I was forced to go down and sit with the girls. As I entered the lower section, both groups of three girls on each side crushed up to make room for me. I chose the left, where I was wedged between a girl called Frances and her two friends. This physical proximity was the best start to the day I had so far experienced, and I realised that Frances was one of the girls I had pretended not to notice, except for my smiling moodily at her on one of the days when I followed the bus on my bike. We chatted and laughed without pause throughout the journey, in contrast to the way I would normally ignore a girl I didn't know whilst waiting at a bus stop, even if we had waited at the same stop for months. I was deeply disappointed when we reached Ash Street traffic lights, for it was there that the High School girls got off. When I returned home in the afternoon, I had no interest at all in attending to my puncture, and the following morning I waited for the bus once again to relive my newly-found adventure.

Day two was just a little different. I went upstairs to the boys' section only to find that there were two spare places. For reasons I am now unable to fathom, I felt obliged to take one of them, rather than go downstairs to Frances and her friends, which I longed to do. I cannot imagine what ethical forces made me pass up this means of satisfying my desires, but I did. For some weeks the frequency of sitting downstairs with the girls was determined entirely by the availability of upstairs spaces, and it was not until I found a little common sense that I submitted to my wishes and joined them as a matter of routine. Much as I loved my bike, I used it only rarely after that until I was bought a new Humber Clipper on entering the Sixth Form. In those earlier days the bus rides with Frances and her friends were joyful and light-hearted, even though they remained unconsummated. For me, a kiss in public on a bus in 1952 was just too daring to contemplate.

My first public kiss was with a girl called Cheryl. On one of the many weekends spent with my cousin John in Stockport, we went train spotting one evening on Warwick Road railway bridge in Heaton Moor. We were joined by John's friends, Ron and Dai, who were pupils at Burnage Grammar School. At the other end of the bridge was a blonde girl smiling at us or, more precisely, at Ron and Dai. She walked over and started talking to us, and it was clear that the two boys had met her before. As John and I were introduced to Cheryl, she made it clear that anyone who wanted a necking session only had to ask. John took up the offer at once, and in no time, the two of them were out of sight behind a large rhododendron bush. I was amazed. I had spent several months working out the preparatory dialogue which I had assumed to be a necessary prelude to kissing. In fact, it bothered me considerably because, although I could imagine my own side of the conversation, I was not equipped to anticipate the girl's part, and so the entire process remained imponderable and other-worldly. After all, I was probably handicapped by not having viewed any romantic films, for there was not much kissing in 'The Three Stooges' and Abbott and Costello. Despite all this, here was a girl who was not only prepared to kiss me, but was actually taking the initiative by inviting me to sample her wares.

John and Cheryl emerged from the bush with red faces and contented smiles. She then glanced in my direction, and this was clearly my cue to enter the rhododendron bush. All my previous worries about negotiating this romantic entanglement dispersed, for Cheryl was clearly an experienced kisser and knew exactly what to do. As they say in the cheap novels, I was 'putty in her hands'. This was complete heaven, heightened by the perfume of Cheryl lipstick which was of a flavour that boiled sweets had not prepared me for. A few days later, with my confidence and self-esteem almost off the top of the scale, I kissed a girl called Jean outside the chip shop on Heaton Road, not caring who was watching. After all this, train spotting lost a little of its magic and life entered a completely new chapter. I had experienced the ecstasy; the agony had yet to be encountered.

PLAYING FOR SPENCER'S

I cannot remember a time when I did not enjoy sport in the winter, although the summer variety was quite a different matter. Football was an all-consuming interest, not just at Prep school, but also during the long hours spent on Bedford Park with friends, kicking a ball until long after the sun had set. I had no enthusiasm at all for cricket, mainly because I possessed no particular skill at the game. This meant that I would be low in the batting order and invariably asked to field somewhere on the boundary. If ever the ball came my way there was an even chance that I would be looking in a different direction, such was my boredom with this activity. Should my inattention cause a catch to be missed, I would rightly suffer the indignation of my team-mates. That kind of rôle in a game that seemed to last almost as long as a Wagner opera is not likely to breed an appetite for more of the same and so, in my later years at KGV, I chose cross-country running as an alternative to cricket, a pastime I found agreeable if not exciting. We ran past the Cox Café Rio at Kew and up to the Isolation Hospital before returning to the school grounds via Kew Woods, where Queenscourt Hospice now stands. This was a solitary activity with a freedom to think whilst running; one I came to enjoy.

The first term at KGV introduced me to many new experiences, one of which was Rugby. Although it never replaced football as my first choice, I did enjoy the sport and was happy to participate as often as I could. During the first season I played in the top group alongside players of considerable talent, like Colin Andrews, Den Dover, Freddie Wilson and

Barrie Whittaker. My particular problem was one of size and, for the first three years there was only one boy in my form, Ian Hill, who was smaller than I was. I played scrum half at the age of eleven and, in the early stages, acquitted myself quite well, but as time went by my lack of stature reduced my effectiveness and I was moved to play on the wing, not as a try scorer of searing pace, but simply as a useful utility player. The following year I was demoted to a group of more moderate ability on games afternoons. Although this ruled out any possibility of playing for the school, it did keep open the opportunity to represent Spencer's at inter-house Rugby competitions.

During my time at the school, Spencer's House excelled at only one sport - swimming. Mike Harris, the captain, was just one of several talented swimmers, and the house collected a number of trophies for the sport, including some for life-saving. There was an expectation at KGV that every boy should be able to swim by the end of his first year, and this accounted for the prominence of the activity in the school's sporting range. Most of us went to the Victoria Baths on the promenade on a regular basis, either straight after school or on Saturday mornings. The Bird Bath was too small for us, but we spent hours and hours in the First Class and the Premier Plunge. We went home with wet hair and smelling of chlorine. In Summer, many of us frequented the Open Air Pool in Princes Park, which was always heaving with people in the holiday season. I recall a day when we were about twelve and discovered the sandpit behind the main colonnades, where middle-aged and elderly men sun-bathed in the nude. Highly excited at this daring prospect, we went and entered the cubicles, removed all our clothes, and ran giggling into the sandpit, diving onto our fronts to hide our microscopic genitalia from public view.

I seem to remember that Spencer's turned out a reasonable cricket team and that my friend Philip McLean was one of the leading lights. In other respects, our performances ranged from moderate to dismal. At the end of the term Mr Marsden would review the Spencer's record and, almost routinely, would observe that, although we had lost x number of games, there was clearly a promise of quality that would "come into its own next year". It never did, at least, not in my time, and the fragility of his prediction was comparable to the forlorn hope that the Conservatives might win the 2001 General Election.

I played Rugby for Spencer's house at the age of fourteen in a team that, as far as I can recall, lost all of its matches. Ian Hill, the captain, was as small as I was, but he was a very good all-round sportsman. Despite my lack of bulk, I could tackle satisfactorily and was able to discharge my duties as scrum half with reasonable skill. Aside from Hill, Burstall and myself, with the addition of promising younger players like

The Premier Plunge at the Victoria Baths

Southport Pier with the Open Air Pool in the background to the left

Burdell, Knowles and Schober, I do not think we frightened the opposition too frequently, despite trying our best. As predicted, we lost all of our games, but our housemaster, loyal and supportive, observed the promise we had shown and the fact that it would doubtless come to fruition in twelve months time. In the sevens competition that followed we actually made a better account of ourselves by winning one game, but we did not progress very far beyond that. So, despite everything, representing Spencer's House at Rugby was my only sporting distinction at KGV. I could not possibly have dreamt that, twenty-five years later, I would be a selector for North of England Schoolboys at the same sport.

19531953195319531953195319531953

SHALL WE DANCE?

For quite some time, Philip McLean and I had concluded that girls were much more interesting than we had initially believed and that the very best way to increase the frequency of our contact with them was to attend the dances at Trafalgar Road Congregational Church Hall. These functions followed a common pattern for those days. There would be about 120 girls and about 30 boys at the dance. For about half of the evening the girls would dance with each other, whilst the boys chatted amongst themselves with their hands in their pockets, just as men do. The music was organised by a middle-aged Master of Ceremonies who was in charge of the gramophone, and who announced the title of each record with a discernible cultural distance from the clientele. It was all a far cry from the anarchistic Rock n' Roll that would change all our lives in about three years time, but we were not to know that. For the last waltz, a big mirror ball would cast moving dots of light into an otherwise dark environment. This was in strong contrast to the bright and revealing lighting that characterised all but this ultimate dance, which was of great symbolic and practical importance for the girls, for none of them wanted to dance bust to bust during this romantic finale, even though many of them had little more pectoral development than we did. The boys were in the happy position of being, like rare stamps, highly collectible. The great benefit of the last waltz was that you walked home the girl you had last danced with. On the first occasion I walked a girl called Pat home to Walmer Road. We kissed at her front door, but it was not French kissing, for neither of us had yet reached that level of experience.

Philip was a much better dancer than I was. He seemed to know the steps to all the popular tunes - quick step, fox trot, slow waltz and samba - as well as to some of the traditional dances such as the St Bernard Waltz, the Barn Dance and the Gay Gordons, the name being still without

74

its more recent associations. As he guided his partner with flourish through a broad range of musical items, I staggered around the dance floor with the best intentions, but the smiles I received from my partners at the end of each ordeal were more of pity and pain than of pleasure and enthusiasm. Because the boys were heavily outnumbered, I was never going to be without a partner, but increasingly my circle was confined to those who were physically more robust and, in particular, those who were wearing sensible shoes.

The one I most wanted to dance with was a girl named Jean, a slim and attractive girl with dark brown hair and a beautiful complexion. She wore delicate high-heeled shoes with dainty silver straps. I decided to make my move when the Master of Ceremonies announced a St Bernard Waltz, for I believed, quite mistakenly as it turned out, that I knew the right steps. I walked across the width of the dance floor and asked her for "the pleasure of the next dance", an unfortunate choice of words as it turned out. In those days girls never refused a request such as this, which was just as well. I often wondered what I would do if a girl ever refused to dance, but I never came up with an answer. We started quite successfully, but as we came to the point where the boy takes two steps backwards and stamps his feet, I forgot about the two steps back and stamped twice - very heavily - on Jean's dainty, silver-strapped high-heeled shoes. I can still see the look of agony on her face as I escorted her to the side of the dance floor. The fact that she was prepared to dance with me again, albeit not on that same evening, said much more for her kindness and resilience, I suspect, than for my irresistible magnetism.

There was now no denying that lessons were necessary. On our road was The Bullen School of Dancing, and my mother offered to speak to Gerald Bullen, who went to Mass at the same church as we did, to see if he could arrange lessons for me at an affordable rate. So it was that at 5.45 on the following Thursday I rang the bell of the School of Dancing at number 24 in anticipation of my first lesson. Mr Bullen, who was a charming man, if a little effeminate, answered the door and asked me to take a seat in the studio. I sat there in my new lovat sports jacket, waiting for Mrs Bullen to arrive. After five minutes. *Mr* Bullen entered the room, put a record on the gramophone, and approached me with his arms raised in what looked to me like a ballet position, saying "Right, Paul, we'll start with the Quick Step". I was mortified! Mr Bullen, performing the female steps, whisked me round the studio to the sound of Victor Sylvester and his Orchestra. What if my friends found out that I had danced with a man? It was all too terrible to contemplate. I would simply have to leave town. Nevertheless, on successive Thursdays, we practised the entire range of modern dances, and I deduce that I emerged from this bizarre and, most fortunately, covert experience slightly more competent than before I began. The main problem was that, although I could dance reasonably well with Mr Bullen leading me, even though I was performing the man's steps, I was much less successful with girls of my own age, where I was expected to take the initiative, so I had still not really found an answer to my problem of terpsichorean inefficiency. However, I stopped short of inviting him to join me at Trafalgar Road Congregational Church Hall!

THE WORLD OF WORK

In the summer holidays after I took O level examinations, my cousin John and I were found temporary work by my Uncle Edgar in the warehouse of McVitie & Price Biscuits in Levenshulme where he was a cost accountant. I suspect that John was under-age, but nobody asked any questions and we were duly issued with caramel-coloured overalls and asked to report to the supervisor. In those days the warehouse was not automated, and so all orders had to be made up manually. Our job was to take an order form with a list of requirements written on it, to push a trolley round the warehouse and to collect whatever tins of biscuits were listed until the order was complete. We then reported back to a senior colleague who would check our efficiency. The biscuits were arranged in stacks that were piled up to ten tins high, and so the warehouse looked a bit like the New York skyline. The safety regulations were either non-existent or unobserved because John and I, along with others, scrambled over the piles of tins like Gibraltar apes to locate the ones we needed.

Inevitably, the day came when an accident happened. I was coming to the end of my list, needing only six tins of Milk Chocolate Home Wheat biscuits to complete the order. These were almost inaccessible because three stillages - big metal-wheeled flat trucks each holding 112 tins - were blocking my way. These particular stillages held Custard Creams which, along with Ginger Nuts, were amongst the heaviest of the biscuits, whereas Appledoorn and Ice Wafers were the featherweights. In order to make a gap to get my trolley through to the Home Wheat, I put my feet on the first of the stillages, braced my back against the wall and pushed as hard as I could. The effect was a bit like the shunting of railway wagons. The first hit the second which hit the third and rebounded off a large pillar. The six-high piles of Custard Creams wobbled before collapsing in a 30-second explosion of crashing that brought every warehouse worker to a halt before they rushed to my aid. Some tins had hit the floor and exploded in a shower of broken biscuits, whilst others turned into polyhedra with the force of the impact. After the main cacophony had ceased there were one or two final 'boings', very much like the sound effects for which the Goon Show became famous on radio.

Mr Edwards, the supervisor, was so horrified that he was unable to speak for a few seconds. Meanwhile, I was miraculously unhurt, whilst my cousin was hiding behind a stack of Bourbon tins in order to conceal his hysterical laughter. I was told firmly that, were I to be charged for the damage, my three weeks wages would not cover the cost. The final tally was eighty-four tins written off and a further sixteen with smashed contents. Occasionally, we would deliberately drop the odd tin so that the workers could nibble the broken biscuits throughout the day, but my escapade was unparalleled in its scale and drama. Surprisingly, I was neither dismissed nor charged for my misdemeanour, but I was most careful with my trolley for the rest of my time at McVitie & Price, moving around the warehouse with a greater sense of caution.

The other paid employment I undertook before I eventually left grammar school was at Pleasureland on the Southport sea front, where I worked really hard over a ten-day period for which I received the sum of two pounds ten shillings. I had not discussed payment with my boss before I started and, as so often happens at that age, I did not think to dispute the small size of my wages until it was too late, and I suppose it is all part of the learning process. My job was to be in charge of the Strikers, where you had to hit a rubber stump with a mallet to make a silver metal arrow travel vertically up a list of prizes. When the arrow stopped, it was up to me to hand over the appropriate prize, which would be similar to those found in Christmas crackers. I suppressed my embarrassment at the disappointment these objects generally caused, and got on with shouting the obligatory slogan: "Try your luck on the Strikers, everybody! A prize every time!" I think I might have worked for a longer period had I not overheard a comment made by a woman as she and her husband passed by my stall one afternoon. "Look at that boy in the KGV blazer working here. I am sure Mr Dixon would be really ashamed to see that." Perhaps she was right in her assessment of the situation. I wore my blazer, partly because dress was not so casual in those days, but mainly it was all I had apart from my new sports jacket. I was considerably more distressed by her chance remark than perhaps I ought to have been but, then, that is the dilemma of the adolescent.

195419541954195419541954195419541954

WAITING FOR A SOUTHPORT BUS

On the basis that it is a good move to pre-empt accusations of personality disorder by confessing to them openly, I willingly admit to having been a nerd as far as bus- and train-spotting is concerned. Although my cousin and I should have outgrown these pastimes by the age of sixteen, our interest was, if anything, even more obsessive. It wasn't that we pursued buses and locomotives as a substitute for chasing girls; we made time for both. So it was that we spent hours and hours in Stockport's Mersey Square, Piccadilly in Manchester, Warwick Road Railway Bridge in Heaton Moor, Bank Quay Station in Warrington, and Chapel Street and Lord Street in Southport, both the roads and the railway stations.

Railway locomotives, and particularly those of the Midland Region, were handsome living creatures. The romance of steam and, in particular, the smell of it, really cannot be exaggerated as a sensory experience. Memorable, too, although not quite so enjoyable, is the stinging of the eyes caused by hot fragments from the chimney whilst looking forwards out of the window on a steam train journey, yet whatever the suffering, it was always worth it. From the age of about ten, we would stand, often with other daft kids, on railways bridges or station platforms with our Ian Allan loco books, in which we underlined in red those locomotives we had seen, or 'copped'. Engines we saw quite often in the Southport area were two members of the Jubilee Class, 'Mars' and 'Dauntless'. Because they were so common, we called them 'stinks', and we booed them as they passed by. Locomotives we had not seen before were greeted with cheers and other displays of ecstasy before we got out our red pens and six-inch rulers.

Although buses were not as spectacular as steam engines, they were more frequent and accessible, and we could ride on them at a quite reasonable expense. As well as noting the make of the chassis and body of each bus, we took pains to record the fleet number, the registration plate, the unladen weight, the date the vehicle was introduced into service, and so on. Just as the ornithologist receives a buzz from sighting rare birds, so we experienced the ecstasy of spotting a bus that had previously eluded our investigation, such as one of the two rarely-seen single-deck Crossleys that Southport Corporation had acquired in 1951. The occasional visits to the bus depot at Canning Road was our equivalent to the birdwatchers' trips to the mud flats at Marshside.

Well, that's it, really. For anyone who is similarly eccentric, I present below the details of the Southport fleet up to 1954 . (A full list of Southport girls of the period, complete with unladen weights, is available on request)

No.	Chassis	Body	Reg.No.	Seat	Intro
1	Vulcan VSD	Vulcan	FY 6272	28	1924
2	AEC 411	Willowbrook	FY 8473	30	1925
3	Vulcan	Vulcan	FY 8492	30	1925

Southport Corporation Daimler with the Trocadero cinema on the right

KGV Model Club with the author second from the right

4	Vulcan VWB	Vulcan	FY 8902	30	1926
5	Vulcan VWBL	Vulcan	FY 8916	30	1926
6-9	Vulcan VWBS	Vulcan	WM 1857-60	32	1928
10-11	Leyland TD1	Leyland	WM 3282-83	51	1929
12	Vulcan Emperor	Vulcan	WM 4961	51	1930
13-22	Vulcan Emperor	Vulcan	WM 5896-05	51	1931
1-4	Vulcan Emperor	Vulcan	WM 5906-9	51	1931
23-28	Leyland TD2	Leyland	WM 7946-51	51	1932
29-48	Leyland TD3	E.E.C.	AFY 957-76	51	1934
49-50	Leyland TD4	Vulcan	CFY 89-90	53	1936
51-55	Leyland TD5c	Massey	CWM 567-71	55	1937
5	Guy Wolf CFP	Guy	BWM 882	20	1949
7	Guy Wolf CFN	Guy	CWM 349	25	1937
56-59	Daimler CWA6	North.Counties	EWM 344-47	56	1944
60-63	Daimler CWA6	Duple	EWM 356-59	56	1945
64-65	Daimler CWA6	Duple	EWM 372-73	56	1945
66-68	Daimler CWD6	Duple	EWM 374-76	56	1945
69-71	Daimler CWA6	Duple	EWM 377-79	56	1945
72-83	Daimler CWA6D	Duple	EWM 541-52	56	1946
1-4	Bedford QL)	Rimmer, Harris	EWM 680-83	23	1946
11-18	Bedford QL)	& Sutherland	FFY 165-72	23	1947
84-95	Leyland PD2/3	Leyland	FFY 401-12	56	1947
96-110	Leyland PD2/3	Leyland	GFY 396-410	56	1950
111	Crossley DD42/7T	Crossley	GFY 411	56	1950
112	Crossley DD42/7S	Crossley	GFY 412	56	1950
113-15	AEC Regent III	Crossley	GFY 413-15	56	1949
116-17	Crossley SD42/7T	Crossley	GWM 816-17	32	1951
20-26	Leyland PD2/12	Weymann	HFY 720-26	58	1952
27-30	Leyland PD2/20	Weymann	KFY 27-30	58	1954

BEING IN THE SIXTH FORM

I entered the Sixth form in 1954 after taking O level in the subjects I would not be sitting at A level, as was the plan for those in the Trans forms. We had the dubious privilege of sitting these examinations one year earlier than everyone else, and my choice for A level, which I had made at the unjustifiably young age of thirteen, was Art, French and Latin. In addition to these three we did two further subjects. The first was Scripture, from which I no longer absented myself as Catholics and Jews were permitted to do. Indeed, I suspect that my lack of formal religious education between the ages of eleven and seventeen did much to prevent me from turning away from Catholicism, which might not have been the case, had I attended a Catholic secondary school. The other lesson was General

Studies, through which I was introduced to the hitherto unexplored and engaging discipline of Syllogistic Logic by Mr Dyer. My interest in the last two lessons was indicative of a growing interest in current affairs, questions of ethics, the purpose of life, and so on. This was also the year that I wrote to the BBC about Graham Sutherland's portrait of Churchill, and glowed with pleasure when the letter was read out on the air, only to be deflated the following week when a listener wrote to describe me as an immature schoolboy who should be spanked and sent to bed. Politics, too, seemed more important than it had been before and so, when I had discovered that the Toldas Group, a pacifist movement that was one of several forerunners of CND, held meetings in Lyndhurst Road, I was keen to join. There seemed to be no age barrier and I was made welcome by others in the group.

Every Thursday at 7 o'clock, for a period of about three months, I went to the house of brother and sister Arthur and Bessie Shipley to take part in debates about nuclear deterrence and related issues. The leader was Professor Alan Litherland who was well versed in the facts and policies surrounding the balance of power in the world. Every so often Arthur's brother Harry would pop up at the meeting and inject his contentious views, to the alarm of some of the more formal members. I had been brought up in a Conservative family, but pacifism seemed to me to transcend party politics. Although it is difficult at sixteen to take an overview of alternative arguments, I was convinced that the belief in making ever-increasing instruments of war in order to attain peace was untenable. As weeks went by I became more vocal in the meetings, assuming a level of confidence that only those with very limited experience can cheerfully sustain. They were kind to me, presumably pleased to have a young member there. At school I joined the Council for Education in World Citizenship and wore my badge with some pride.

One of the great benefits of a grammar school sixth form in those days was the availability of diverse occupations open to us all, in addition to our academic work. I continued with my commitment to the School Choir, adding the Madrigal Group to my list; I became a regular attender and sometime contributor to the Debating Society; I sustained my interest in cross-country running; I was a keen member of the team that painted sets for the school plays and I appeared on stage in 'Romeo and Juliet', admittedly in a minor rôle. Much time was also spent in the forming and running of the Model Club of which I was secretary and, later, chairman. From the age of seven I had developed an unaccountably strong interest in the making of model theatres, not so much because of an interest in drama, but more related to a fascination with operating curtains and lighting and, when older, with the construction of a revolving stage. I made my very last theatre at the age of 29!

As part of our educational development we were taken on visits to the theatre. One of our set books for A level French was 'Les Femmes Savantes' by Moliere, and were were taken to a performance of the play at the David Lewis Theatre in Liverpool. Every summer George Wakefield, the Head of English, organised a two-day visit to Stratford-upon-Avon so that we could experience Shakespeare in the finest possible setting. In 1954 and 1955 we saw a total of four productions: 'Othello', 'A Midsummer Night's Dream', Macbeth' and 'Twelfth Night'. I missed a large part of the last of these due to falling asleep in the heat of the upper balcony. When I awoke, an Aero chocolate bar had melted in the pocket of my KGV Old Boys blazer - which we were permitted to wear a few weeks before leaving - and I never quite got rid of the chocolate as long as I owned the garment. To my lasting shame, I threw the glutinous contents of the pocket out of the window of Gore's coach as we left Stratford. It splattered the windscreen of a car being washed by an unfortunate man, whose expression as the chocolate hit its target resembled that of 'The Scream' by Edvard Munch. A Shakespearean tragedy, indeed.

One of the more appetising items on the calendar was the annual debate with the Southport High School for Girls, usually held in their hall. The subject of the last debate I attended was 'That Beauty nowadays is more important than Brains'. We looked forward to this with the kind of uncontrollable excitement found only in single-sex schools. Although we wanted to be in the presence of girls as often as possible, we knew very little about the way they thought. More to the point, we had the most obtuse notions about what might make us even more attractive to the opposite sex than we were already. These considerations presented us with the dilemma of choosing between contradictory behaviours. Should we be decisive and dominant or tender and considerate? Would they prefer us serious and scholarly or crazy and adventurous? How much Brylcreem is about right? Is it better to squeeze a spot or leave it? Are you more desirable with glasses or without, particularly if you are prone to falling downstairs in the dark? We had not yet reached that level of maturity where we understood, firstly, that most girls think as individuals and do not possess a homogeneous view and, secondly, that we would probably be far more successful and save ourselves hours of worry and preparation if we were simply to be ourselves. This, of course, was too lofty a concept at that stage in our development.

Although Trafalgar Road Congregational Church Hall dances had served us well in the past, our attention turned now to parties. We regarded them as more sophisticated and, for me, they lessened the chances of maiming someone to whom I was attracted by stamping on their toes. Phil McLean and I were diligent party-goers, and one of our favourite venues was the basement flat on Manchester Road where Philip's girl friend Monica Wilson, known as 'Honk', lived with her mother. At that point in the mid-1950s most of our friends were either from KGV or the High School, and those we saw at nearly every party were Barbara Agar, Heather Brayshaw, Valerie Kelly, Barbara Devitt and probably quite a few others whose names do not come to mind. All of this was part of the induction process into young adulthood, and I must say that I found this post-adolescent phase a happy and fulfilling experience.

The other interest Philip and I shared was classical music, and we would often meet at his home on Liverpool Road to listen to Mendelssohn and Beethoven on his Pye Black Box record player. Sometimes, when no-one was around, we would conduct the music with knitting needles, turning over the pages of our score - the Radio Times - with a flourish evocative of Sir Thomas Beecham. Because of limited spending power, I still had to soldier on with a second-hand wind-up gramophone, but this in no way reduced my musical interest. However, a little of the magic is lost when a symphony is recorded onto the eight sides of four 78 rpm records. Since I could afford to buy only one record per month from Allan Smith's on Eastbank Street or Aldridges on Hoghton Street, my collection was built very slowly. None of this dampened my enthusiasm, and one of my proudest moments was being asked to present a selection of my favourite music to the Southport Gramophone Society at the invitation of the Chairman, Mr Howgate, who was my mother's banking adviser at the Westminster in Birkdale.

Pop music was something that held no interest for me until the middle of the 1950s. I developed a liking for the voice of David Whitfield, partly because he sounded slightly operatic, but mainly because I discovered some success in imitating him. Whilst my mother was out, I would sing 'Cara Mia' and 'Answer Me' in front of my wardrobe mirror, unaware that in a few years time I would be doing the same with a guitar and a mean expression. Of course, popular music has a capacity for reminding us all of holidays, parties, romances and so on, in a way that serious music rarely does. The principal pop singers when I was in the Sixth Form were Frankie Laine, Johnny Ray and Guy Mitchell. Johnny Ray's recording of 'Such a night' was banned by the BBC because it was considered suggestive, containing, as it did, unmistakable rhythmic grunts of sexual intercourse. Needless to say, the ban guaranteed the record's success, just as later ones would do for a number of artists, including the Sex Pistols and Frankie Goes To Hollywood.

My mother and I may not have been able to afford many luxuries at this time, but things were beginning to look up. Strange to relate, it was 1954 before rationing finally came to an end. Then, families were no longer restricted in the quantities they were able to buy. Although I had not yet acquired a radiogram that would play LP records - that was to come on my eighteenth birthday - I did have a suit, a new bike with a speedometer, and suede shoes. Above all, we were now on the telephone, a major step forward in telecommunications, even though we had to keep an eye on how often we used it. It is strange to recollect that we still did not possess a television in those days, and I can remember going to the house of friends of ours, Mr and Mrs Carter of Central Avenue, to watch on their huge 17" black and white television set the 1954 Football World Cup, in which Hungary, clearly the best team in the world, were defeated by West Germany in the final.

The most misguided purchase I made in those days was a pipe. I had never smoked cigarettes before, let alone pipe tobacco, but my cousin and I went into Southport where I chose a stylish model as my first introduction to the sophisticated world of the pipe smoker. We then went to a tobacconist in London Street to complete the purchase. I asked a lady with artificially bright red hair to recommend a brand of pipe tobacco. "This is very popular", she responded, handing me a packet of Condor Thick Twist. John and I returned home on the bus to try out this new and highly motivating acquisition. I had great difficulty in preparing the tobacco for insertion into the bowl of the pipe, for it was a thick plug in the shape of a small cigar. After much chopping with a penknife, I finally filled the bowl and lit a match. The first attempt had to be aborted because I had packed the tobacco so tightly that I almost damaged my ear drums as I tried in vain to suck air through the mouthpiece. After more adjustments, success was achieved as I drew a long breath of smoke into my mouth. "Honey sweet"' I remarked as I passed the pipe to John so that he could share my ecstasy. One was enough for him, but I carried on in a determination to get my money's worth out of the tobacco. My cousin then pointed out that, although we sometimes describe people as 'going green', I had...quite literally. We all have to vomit at some point in our lives, but there have been very few occasions when I have retched as badly as on that day. The 'honey sweet' Condor remained untouched for six months, sold to me by a red-rinsed woman who knew exactly what she was doing!

In the KGV sixth form I managed to do a little growing up, to make good friends and to enjoy the privilege of being taught by men of distinct talent. Relationships with other boys were more relaxed and less silly. We dropped nicknames in favour of Christian names and we began to display that rarest of virtues in teenage boys, tolerance. I made friendships then which have proved durable, despite an infrequency of contact in many cases. These would include Stan Rimmer, with whom I continue to work very closely on the Old Georgians' Association Committee, comprising former pupils of King George V School and former students of KGV College; John Hoyle, my solicitor; Stan Roberts, a lifelong friend since we studied A level Art together; Roger Hargreaves, whose father was a distinguished teacher at KGV; and Philip McLean, to whose younger son I am Godfather, and who married Dorothy, daughter of our Latin master, Robert Kirkby.

There were some amazing characters on the staff of KGV in my day. One of these was Joe Charnley, known as 'Froggy' because he taught French, who possessed a most amazing skill. He was able to jump with his feet together from the floor onto the master's desk, and this when he was in his late fifties. Quite why he did it was something of a mystery, but it certainly impressed us because those of us who tried to imitate him invariably ended up with badly bruised shins. Another member of the French department was George 'Duckie' Drake, whom we treated most unkindly when I think back. He wore a hearing aid, and the trick we played was to mime our answers to his questions so that he would deduce that his aid needed the volume turning up. When he did this, we spoke in abnormally loud voices, to our amusement and to his discomfort. Our other technique was to make a corporate humming sound to deceive Mr Drake into believing that the hearing aid batteries were misfunctioning. I am now most ashamed of our behaviour towards this kind and inoffensive man.

Teachers whose influence I valued were my first form master, Hubert Evans, Cliff Flemming a kind and gentle man who was my form master in Trans Y, my housemaster, Bill Marsden, John Waddington, under whose guidance I developed a lifelong passion for the visual arts, and George Wakefield, quite simply the best teacher I had and to whom I dedicate the following chapter. I would add to this list Hubert Long who, although he did not teach me, became a close and valued friend from the mid-1980s when we served together on the Old Georgians committee until his death in 2000, and Geoffrey Dixon, the headmaster who started at KGV when I did in 1949, and with whom I have enjoyed a warm relationship now that I am no longer afraid of him.

I WISH I'D SAID THAT TO HIM
(Extract from the Red Rose 2001 - Stories of KGV)

A DfEE recruitment campaign in 1999 proclaimed that 'no-one forgets a good teacher'. Without any doubt, the finest teacher I encountered in my time as a schoolboy at KGV was George Wakefield. He possessed the skill of being able to make people work from enthusiasm and stimulation, rather than from duress. He gave me - and probably all of us - a reverence for, and a ready appreciation of, the written word. This process was assisted by a sense of humour. Once, George was to arrive a few minutes late for our English lesson in Lower VX. Whilst we were waiting, Leslie Ashworth took the opportunity to launch a paper aeroplane across the room. As the aircraft left his hand, George swept into the room with his gown flowing and with his idiosyncratic limping stride. Most other teachers would almost certainly have screamed, "Ashworth! What on earth do you think you're doing? Get out!" George, without even glancing at the culprit, announced, "for your imposition, Ashworth, you will write me an essay on aeronautics. Now, will you all open your books at page twenty-seven?" Ashworth had been reprimanded, but not demeaned; we had been amused, yet deterred. No blood had been shed.

I made a decision whilst still quite young that I wanted to be a teacher, and I now know that this early choice was the right one. If anyone at King George V School influenced my aspiration, it was GPW, and there were several occasions during my time as a teacher when I thought of George and his capacity to inspire; his natural talent for combining warmth with firmness; his infectious enthusiasm; his appetite for getting things right; his style. His dedication was shown clearly in the plays he produced at the school over a long period. Geoffrey Dixon once remarked that George's production of Hamlet in 1952 was comparable in its treatment with that of a professional company, and that it matched a performance he had seen recently in the West End. Quite clearly, those who attended these dramas were aware that they witnessed more than just the kind of school play for which one must make generous allowances. George managed to draw more from his young actors than even they thought they could achieve, and he did this by understanding, not just the subtleties of drama, but also the working of the young mind. Perhaps his finest quality was the retaining of the memory of just what it was like to be a teenager, a prerequisite for anyone wishing to work effectively in the secondary sector.

I may well not have been among George Wakefield's most distinguished pupils, but I was certainly one of his greatest admirers. I met him on several occasions after I left, but sadly not often enough to get to know him as well as I should have wished. When we spoke, his interest in the progress of my own career always seemed genuine. The last occasion I saw him was in 1988, not long after a BBC2 '40 minutes' television programme that featured an exchange between sixth formers at my own school in Kirkby and those at the prestigious Rugby School had been shown. I recall George complimenting me generously on my contribution to the programme, and my appreciation of his praise was in proportion to the esteem in which I held him. I did not meet him again before he died. I later told June, his widow, that George had been by far the most influential and charismatic of all those who had taught me. I only wish I'd said that to him.

NEW DOORS OPENING

Art was one of my three A level subjects, those we did not have to sit at O level. It was clear from the age of twelve that this would be my main subject, and the one which might well determine my career. At fourteen I had decided that my future was to be in architecture, unaware that its scientific nature demanded A levels in Maths and Physics. When I discovered this, my interest turned to teaching, for a number of reasons. Firstly, I found that I had a good rapport with younger boys in my house, in the Model Club and in the choir. Secondly, I had the greatest regard for two of my teachers, John Waddington and George Wakefield, who seemed to me to personify the attributes of the ideal teacher. My father, a teacher himself, would not have wished me to enter the profession and had hoped that I would make a career in the law. Perhaps, if I had continued at Alderwasley and then moved on to public school, his wish might have been granted, for I doubt whether A level Art would have been encouraged strongly at most of the major independent Catholic schools in the 1950s.

To be able to involve myself in art for almost a quarter of the week was to be in paradise. In those days the numbers were quite small, so we had plenty of room and adequate individual attention. Meunier and Sutton were in the Upper Sixth and appeared highly talented to us. My own year included Stan Roberts, Donald Holt and Bob Hewett, with the addition of Brian Geldard later in the year. For much of the time, John Waddington was teaching a junior group whilst we had the senior art room to ourselves. He would make visits to monitor our progress, but we enjoyed quite a measure of freedom and, as long as our work rate was satisfactory, we were free to talk about anything we wished, crack jokes, mimic members of staff and indulge in other silly behaviour consistent with our level of immaturity. Once, Geoffrey Dixon came into the room just as Stan Roberts was teaching me the tango. He was not amused.

Halfway through the year Bryan Geldard arrived. He was a dour yorkshire boy with a sense of fun, but no wish to exert himself in A level Art. He added an extra flavour to the humour in the lessons and was popular with the rest of us. There was a stockroom attached to the senior art room and, from time to time, Bryan would lock himself in, refusing to open the door to the rest of us. It may be that he wanted a smoke, but we were never sure because there was a window in the room through which he could have disposed of any evidence. Once in a while I would bang on the door authoritatively and shout, "Geldard! Open this door!" in an imitation of headmaster, Geoffrey Dixon. Geldard was never fooled and simply shouted back, "Bugger off, Bagshaw!".

Then, one day, when Geldard had once again barricaded himself in this small room, denying us access to art materials, the main door opened and Geoffrey Dixon, gowned and dignified, entered the room. He moved slowly round in the manner of a hunting shark, pausing to look at our paintings as we worked with an intensity rarely displayed. "Is anyone absent?" he asked. *"No sir"* we replied. "I thought there were five of you," he said. *"Yes sir."* "Who is missing?" *"Geldard, sir."* The tension was building. "Where is Geldard?" *"He's in the stockroom, sir."* We held our breath as the headmaster moved smoothly across to the stockroom and turned the handle of the door. It was locked. The dream sequence continued. "Geldard! Open this door!" *"Bugger off, Bagshaw!"* screamed Geldard, starting, if he only knew it, to write his own leaving note. "Geldard, if you don't unlock this door immediately I shall get a caretaker to force it open!" Now, come out at once!" There was a brief silence while Geldard pondered on the authenticity of what he had just heard. It was very good; just like the real thing. Perhaps it was the real thing. Unable to take the risk, Bryan Geldard opened the door of the stockroom to face the silhouette of a stern figure glowering at him. Batman wins again. It is sad to report that, only a few weeks after this incident, Geldard left King George V School, and one of our more colourful colleagues was with us no longer.

I admired greatly our art teacher, John Waddington. His drawing skills seemed to my teenage eye as bordering on genius, and his teaching technique was natural and relaxed. He wasn't the stereotypical arty type at all, for everything in the department was well organised and efficiently arranged. Most important of all, he did not convey the impression, as some art teachers do, that he was there simply to earn a living and that the main priority was the creative pursuit of his own art work. His lessons were orderly and purposeful, yet I never remember an occasion when he raised his voice. Although I had not been conscious of it at the time, I believe that my own approach to running an art department in the 1960s embraced some of the principles that John Waddington established at KGV. To our dismay, he left the school at the end of our lower sixth year to become Art Adviser to the Cheshire Education Authority. By then, we were on course for passing A level with reasonable comfort, and his successor, Norris Harrison, simply had to ensure that we remained dedicated to our tasks.

As I became more deeply absorbed in the production of my own art work, I was increasingly conscious of influences from the work of great artists. At fourteen, I regarded Raphael as the absolute peak of artistic achievement, but this inspiration was counter-productive because his art and my art were so far apart in sheer quality that I was faced with an unattainable aspiration. A little later, on my first attempt at oil painting, I executed a copy of a picture by Edouard Manet, and I received a measure of encouragement from learning about an alternative means of representation. Then, a new and unexpected interest arrived with my purchase of a small book on the post-impressionist painter Paul Gauguin, whose works, with their linear curves and their dazzling colours, aroused an appetite for the exotic. For some months after this, I was mesmerised by the effects of using orange, yellow, lime green and viridian green in still life paintings which, although I had not fully realised it, owed much in their style of representation to the synthetic cubist paintings of Picasso. Other experiments involved me in works displaying semi-abstract city-scapes or interiors with views through doorways and windows, all of which adopted an approach similar to stage design, but retained the Gauguin colouring. The most pretentious designs I remember creating were my own highly-coloured abstract visual equivalents of symphonic music, inspired by a romantic schoolboy belief in the unity of the arts.

Although I could have taken the opportunity for a third year in the Sixth Form, having gained a year by being expressed, I very much wanted to move on to art school which, in 1955, I did, accompanied by my friend Stan Roberts, Donald Holt following a year later. By qualifying for a major bursary from the Southport Education Committee, I enhanced the prospect of being able to remain in full-time education for a further five years and this, along with the death of 82-year-old Auntie Lucy in the same year, guaranteed that my mother and I could manage to live satisfactorily, if not extravagantly, during this period, just as long as my mother remained in part-time employment.

As I left King George V School in the summer of 1955, I was conscious of having completed an educational experience of the very highest quality, although I certainly did not realise how well-prepared and well-equipped we all were to face the future, no matter how out of touch we may have been with the many characteristics of everyday life. Nor did I anticipate that, more than fifty years after starting at the school, I would retain an untarnished affection for the place and the many boys and teachers I met there. The Old Georgians Association, to which over two thousand of us belong, is not just food for a nostalgic appetite; it is a strong and growing organisation with two purposes: to support the present College, and to provide communication and social interactivity amongst those many boys, as well as girls, who have passed through that institution called KGV. Five of us are presently on the governing body of King George V College, and the most encouraging aspect of our Association is that it is expanding year on year, not least as a result of the Old Georgians' section of the College internet website: kgv.ac.uk 'Discipuli Picturam Spectate', as it says in Latin for Today.

PART FOUR
TOWARDS THE END OF FREEDOM
1955-60

BRAVE NEW WORLD
EATING OUT
LEARNING THE GAME
IT'S ONLY ROCK N' ROLL
SUN AND SMOKE
GUILTY BY ASSOCIATION
LOOKING BACK IN ANGER
MAKING AN EXHIBITION
A MATTER OF LIFE AND DEATH
SITTING WITH THE STRANGLERS
TWENTY-ONE TODAY
PUTTING ON THE STYLE
THE OTHER SIDE OF THE BAR
AS ONE DOOR CLOSES
PRACTISING THE ART
CATCHING THE DISEASE
THE END OF FREEDOM
POSTSCRIPT

195519551955195519551955195519551955

BRAVE NEW WORLD

The most dramatic difference for me between KGV and Southport Art School was that the first was for boys only and the second was mixed. No matter how much friendship existed between boys, they were practised in the art of putting each other down and in scoring points, as well as in embarrassing and ridiculing. We simply had to learn to accept this, just as we had great delight in dishing it out. Girls were so kind and civilised by comparison. They appreciated the qualities of others, paid compliments, smiled warmly rather than menacingly, were tolerant, and were quick to offer help whenever it was needed. This was demonstrated at a very early stage by Angela Cubbon, the first girl I spoke to on entering the Southport Art School in September 1955. Girls had no shortcomings at all, or so I initially believed.

Part of my preparation for this new artistic world was the discarding of my blazer in favour of something more casual. It was the age of sloppy sweaters and suede shoes, and nearly all of the male students in our group expressed their individuality by conforming to that image. Next,

90

there was another item of unimposed uniform that we had to possess: the duffel coat. I chose mine from Greenwood's men's outfitters in the Cambridge Arcade, and I was smugly satisfied with the air of classless nonchalance and creative casualness it gave me. The only problem was that my mother insisted on accompanying me to the shop, although I suppose she had some right to be there since she was paying for it. I had to turn round so that she could view the garment from every possible angle, but everything went uneventfully until we left the shop. As I paraded along the arcade in my new duffel coat with its shamefully-clean toggles, reluctantly walking alongside my mother, although trying as hard as I could to appear as though we were not together, two youths of my age leered at me and, in amused mockery, shouted "Mummy bought it for him!"

Apart from lessons in the Use of English and occasional Current Affairs sessions, all our time was spent on studying art - drawing, painting, history of art, anatomy, clay modelling, offset printing and, my own chosen craft, hand-drawn lettering. The only discipline that made us slightly apprehensive in that induction week was life drawing or, more precisely, the confronting for the first time of a nude model. My own way of coping was to stare at the model and nowhere else, just in case someone was watching me watching them watching me. The novelty soon wore off as life drawing became a matter of routine, and I think we were helped by the fact that our first model was at least twenty years older than we were.

Over the years, models of all shapes and sizes came and went. At one end of the scale was Val, only a year or two older than ourselves and most attractive. She stayed for just one term and, when she left, we went to Woolworth's self-service sweet counter and bought her a cavernous bag of assorted sweets, specially chosen for their visual appeal. She was delighted with the present, and I can still see the multi-coloured reflection on her face as she peered into the bag. By contrast, we later had a square-shouldered model called Lottie, who seemed in permanent pain as she posed for us, judging by her grimacing face. She dressed in a grey overcoat with broad shoulder pads and with a metal chain around the waist, giving her the appearance of an East German espionage agent. She was continuously apprehensive of someone peering over the cubicle as she changed, a strange fear for someone who posed naked, or so we thought. It transpired that she had undergone a traumatic experience at another college with a student called 'Hairy' whose behaviour was the source of her anxiety. It was the belief that Hairy would one day return that left her in this troubled state.

There was quite a wide range of students in our year, but not too many were from Southport. Mickey Clough, Cyril Brew and Geoff Turner - known to everybody as 'Tradge' - came from Preston, Heather Pattison was from Crosby, and Carol Hutchinson and Eric Appleton from Ormskirk. The locals were myself and Stan Roberts, my close friend from KGV, Brian Lewis who was to become an equally close friend, and Adrian Greenbank who, like Tradge, later emigrated to Canada. We all got on well, just as most young people who hardly know each other strike up an effortless rapport, principally because they all want to be well thought of by others. The other feature of our lives was the relative freedom we enjoyed compared with what had gone before. If anyone supposed that this relaxed regime was likely to make us lazy, they would be correct, but I don't suppose we differed greatly from most other students of that period.

We were extremely fortunate in the staff we had at the Art School. John Macken, a charming and gentle man, taught us art history, whilst Frank Bass, who was equally pleasant, was our life drawing tutor. Raymond Geering, a man noted for his craftsmanship and precision, imparted to us the subtleties of lettering and typography, and Donald Howarth taught us lithography in his own engaging and unconsciously humorous way. Monty Siroto taught pottery and ceramics, whilst David Harrison took us for pictorial composition. Initially, we thought he was something of a dilettante, but we were mistaken. It is probably true to say that David, as President of the Palette Club, has done more to encourage amateur artists in Southport than anyone else. Later we discovered, to our surprise, that he had performed an act of great courage during the second world war. Harry Ratcliffe, our Principal, exercised authority on the odd occasion it was required, but always in a kindly, paternal way, and we respected him greatly. This was the new world into which we had entered and, for the most part, it was a most attractive one.

EATING OUT

The Art School refectory was fine for routine meals and snacks, and for some time we existed on a diet of beans on toast or welsh rarebit followed by wagon wheels and weak coffee, served by Rusty, our friendly and extravert catering worker. Inevitably, the day came when we decided to be more adventurous, even though it would often cost us more than we could afford. A number of ethnic restaurants serving business meals were opening in Southport, and we chose 'The Oriental' - an odd name for a Greek Cypriot restaurant - in Avondale Road where Brian, Stan, Tradge and I could get a three course lunch for two shillings and sixpence. Jackie, the swarthy proprietor greeted us warmly every day with "'Ello genelmen. 'Ow-are-you-today?" The restaurant was reassuringly dark inside and had soft maroon imitation leather armchairs at round tables. The menu had little choice, but it did change from day to day. A typical meal would consist of chicken soup, which had a mild chicken flavour but otherwise no evidence of chicken, and a bread roll, and the main course might be mixed grill followed by apple pie and custard or rice pudding with jam in the middle. Coffee, if you wanted it, cost extra. The great attraction was the atmosphere of quiet relaxation, which meant that we were frequently late back for the afternoon session.

A more stimulating eating place was the Guest House pub on Union Street, only a five minute walk from the Art School on Mornington Road. Here you could drinks pints - or halves if you were broke - of Draught Bass with the best crusty cheese or ham rolls in Southport. Our regular local pub was 'The Albert', just a short walk along Scarisbrick Street and into London Street, provocatively located next door to the Temperance Institute. If you were really hard up, two of you could share a half of mild and make it last for at least twenty minutes. It sounds strange today to remember that we were not particularly obsessed with alcohol and, in general, we did not go into pubs until we were eighteen, and even then only occasionally. There was a much more seductive and fashionable drink for students in the late 1950s - espresso coffee.

Just as the generation before us had frequented milk bars, so we gathered at coffee bars and, in particular, the El Cabala - now strangely called the 'Gallary Grill' - in Eastbank Street. Everybody wanted to meet there and be seen there. It was a cult, just as was the drinking of the Cappuccino coffee from that dramatic, steaming Gaggia machine, espresso being too strong and bitter for most tastes. My own aspiration at eighteen was to park a Triumph TR2 sports car outside the El Cabala and to saunter casually in with a beautiful girl on my arm, to the admiration of friends and contemporaries. This dream was the perfect case study for 'Putting on the style', an enormous hit for Lonnie Donegan a few years later. Another of our venues was Andy's, a small snack bar in Kingsway on the side of the Garrick Theatre - soon to become the Essoldo cinema - but we went more often to Uncle Mac's, opposite the Promenade Hospital on the corner of Seabank Road, partly because it had a slightly seedy atmosphere, but mainly because it had become fashionable for no particular reason, as so often happens with the tastes of young people.

If this lifestyle sounds pleasantly unadventurous, that is because it was. We had few cares, apart from a shortage of money, and we got on with appreciating each other's company and enjoying our art environment in a naively satisfied way, and with a good deal less of the cynicism that characterises contemporary society. That Dickie Valentine topped the hit parade, both at the beginning of 1955 with 'Finger of Suspicion', and at the end with 'Christmas Alphabet', illustrates the prevailing mood quite eloquently. The brooding heaviness of rock n' roll, the radical anger of social realism, and the stark eccentricity of the beatnik generation had not yet really touched us. Nor, indeed, had the angst of broken relationships, but that was not so very far away.

1956195619561956195619561956195619561956

LEARNING THE GAME

Whenever I hear the song 'It's Almost Tomorrow' by the Dreamweavers, which, I have to admit, is hardly ever, I receive a wave of anguish from the ecstasy and agony of a student love affair that began and ended in the early part of 1956. I must not now identify the chief players in the drama, but I can tell the story. This new girlfriend was quite perfect, occupying my thoughts throughout every hour of the day. It is more than likely that, having come from a boys' school, I was much more susceptible to being swept off my feet than might otherwise have been the case, but here was an occasion when I was smitten and I knew it. We gazed at each other like two goldfish at every opportunity - in the life drawing class, in the refectory, on the stairs, in the corridor. Nothing else in my life mattered, and one of the most gratifying aspects of our affair was that she had given up a boyfriend of twenty-two - yes, a mature adult - in order to be with me. Life was idyllic on a level I had not thus far enjoyed, but that was partly because I had little idea of how to deal with the opposite sex, and my approaches were characterised by naivety and inexperience. Never had Valentine's Day assumed such importance in my calendar.

One evening, about three months into our relationship, we walked together on the Promenade towards the Ribble bus stop at the Floral Hall, from were she would travel home. Our timing was not quite right, and the bus passed us about a quarter of a mile from the stop. I clearly saw the face of a young man on the top deck staring at us and, then, rising from his seat and running downstairs. As this happened, I felt my girlfriend's body stiffen, but when I asked why, there was no answer. The bus stopped at the Floral Hall and the figure we had seen at the window alighted and started walking purposefully towards us. At this point, she admitted that it was her former boyfriend, the one whom I had assumed was part of history. He confronted us, grabbed her arm, told me to find another girl, and the two of them disappeared into the darkness, leaving me standing paralysed on an empty pavement. During this denouement I had neither moved nor spoken. I was in a state of complete inertia and deep shock, just like the proverbial rabbit in the car headlights. I walked home - all two and a half miles - went to bed and cried until I finally fell asleep.

The next day I could neither eat nor think, but I went into college, only to discover that my rival from the previous night was coming in to see me at lunch time. Despite the urge to run away from what I fully expected

94

to be a violent confrontation with someone five years older, I somehow kept myself together and waited for the moment of truth to arrive. To my utter surprise and palpable relief, the conversation was a calm analysis of how we had both been innocent victims of circumstance, and that we must learn from the experience. She deserved neither of us, I was told, and I nodded vigorously, relieved that none of my blood looked like ending up on the carpet. It must be said that being spared physical attack was no compensation for the deep emotional wound, which remained open and painful for months afterwards. Here, if I only realised, was one of life's real lessons, part of a process through which we all must pass. I confided my feelings of desolation to my friend. He told me not to waste my time worrying because she wasn't worth it. What the hell did he know? He married her!

As months passed I had a number of brief relationships with other girls at the Art School, but they were somehow incomplete and second-best. Each, in its own way, was enjoyable and touching but, without exception, I thought of her when I was holding them, and I absorbed the lesson then of how powerful rejection can be, and how the pain it inflicts takes much longer than expected to heal. Since I had not encountered emotional turmoil of this kind before, I was quite unequipped to deal with it. As the Buddy Holly song so accurately tells: "When you love her and she doesn't love you, that's when you're learning the game".

IT'S ONLY ROCK N' ROLL
Dickie Valentine couldn't stay at number one for ever, for which we must all be grateful, but the record that both preceded and succeeded it at the top of the hit parade was unexpected, raucous, aggressive and, to our parents, quite shocking. Bill Haley's 'Rock around the Clock' first came to public notice as the theme tune for the film 'Blackboard Jungle', which depicted violence in American schools, and when youngsters at the cinemas started rioting and causing damage in response to this new sound, there was the beginning of a realisation that major cultural changes were on the way.

It is hard to exaggerate the impact this music made on mid-1950s society, mainly because young people had rarely before possessed a lifestyle that was exclusive. Particularly for boys, maturity was expressed by the adoption of whatever your father, your uncle or your elder brother did and thought and wore. Suddenly, those old rules no longer applied because teenagers had inherited their own music, and with it came their own fashions and their own idiomatic language. Of course, these trappings were all the more desirable because they brought with them adult disapproval, an important precondition of the newly-discovered youth culture. The only other kind of music good for jiving before Rock n' Roll was

Traditional Jazz, which was generally what was played at dances where a live band was appearing. One of our local jazz bands was the Merseysippi Jazzmen, who still continue to play at the Hesketh Arms in Churchtown on Wednesday evenings, attracting enthusiastic fans from all over West Lancashire.

Teddy Boys, with draped jackets and velvet collars, tapered trousers, boot-lace ties, luminous socks, crepe-soled shoes and DA haircuts, along with the violence of Rock n' Roll, represented the new threat to social order, and even if you didn't really want to join in the violence, you couldn't resist the excitement that it generated. The biggest star in the firmament was not, of course, the relatively middle-aged Bill Haley, but Elvis Presley. In view of his gigantic popularity, it is surprising to note that he had only two number one hits in this country between May 1956 and Easter 1959: "All shook up" and "Jailhouse Rock". The first we heard of him was in "Heartbreak Hotel", a tragic and almost incoherently sung rendition of how awful life can be when a relationship ends, something I had recently come to understand only too well. Elvis first recorded at the studio of Sam Phillips who owned Sun Records. Not long before they met, Phillips had been heard to say, "What I need is a white boy who can sing coloured." Indeed, many of those who heard Elvis Presley before they saw him assumed from his voice that he was black. As well as the provocative voice, there was a great controversy surrounding his gyrating pelvic movements on stage. A California policeman observed that "If he did that on the street, we'd arrest him!"

The voice of Elvis was captivating and the sentiments, at least to boys of our age, were resonant. Here was a new way to attract girls, not by smiling, but by adopting an air of menace by glowering moodily at the object of your affection. This, we thought, made us dangerous to know, but it might also attract sympathy, as well as a wish to help and understand our tortured souls. There was a flavour of martyrdom in the role-play, no doubt related to the death in a car crash of the 24-year-old film star, James Dean, only nine months before. "Death is the only thing left to respect," he said, "The one inevitable, undeniable truth." It was the age of the anti-hero, one of the most successful being Marlon Brando, but where Dean was often the vulnerable loser in his films, Brando was the ruthless winner. Many people, including teenagers, could not accept this new attitude and very much wished to preserve the warm, generous and sunny temperament it threatened to replace. For them there was the non-smoking and non-drinking Pat Boone, as wholesome as American apple pie, who sang melodic and agreeable tunes like "I'll be home" and "Friendly Persuasion". If Elvis was the baddy, Pat Boone was the goody, and thus the customary polarisation that occurs periodically in popular taste - the Beatles versus the Stones; Oasis versus Blur - threw up another pair to choose between. Only later did we find out that, in private life, Elvis Presley was a God-fearing Southern boy with high morals and old-fashioned courtesy.

Two new skills were now necessary: to be able to jive and to possess a guitar. For the first, there was no point in returning to Mr Bullen, helpful though he had been in the past. We just had to assimilate this new ritual by watching others and trying our best, and my heart goes out to those poor girls who had to put up with this period of male apprenticeship, for the sake of which they were literally thrown around the dance floor. The second was much more of a problem. Acting out the role of the rock guitarist with a yard brush in front of the wardrobe mirror with a record playing in the background was all very well for personal gratification, but you couldn't really do it in public. Then, something quite wonderful happened: skiffle.

Just as almost anyone could play punk rock in the mid-1970s, so skiffle had that wide accessibility that enabled all of us to participate. If you weren't able to sing or to play the guitar, you could take up the tea chest bass or the washboard or the kazoo, or even build an instrument of your own to add to the texture. The music was a strange mixture of country, folk and jazz and, for a while, it was universally popular, not least because it raised the status of the amateur. The king of skiffle was Lonnie Donegan, who managed to win chart success in the USA as well as in this country, an achievement very few British singers enjoyed. He originally played banjo in Chris Barber's Jazz Band, but our introduction to him as a solo singer was in 'Rock Island Line' at the beginning of 1956. He went on to have a string of hit records on both sides of the Atlantic, including 'Cumberland Gap', 'Putting on the Style', 'Tom Dooley' and 'Does your Chewing Gum Lose Its Flavour'. We were delighted, mainly because you could play almost all of these on the guitar with just three chords.

SUN AND SMOKE

For much of the time at Art School we were encouraged to go out sketching as a means of visual research for the paintings we would later produce in the studio. Because we would have to show the results of our enquiries when we returned, it was rarely possible to get away with taking a few hours completely off work. With this in mind, we spent our time making detailed drawings of the iron tracery under the pier or rowing boats on the Marine Lake or some of the rides at Pleasureland. Nevertheless, we always managed to make time for an ice-cream, a coffee or a hot chocolate before going back, and it is fair to say that outdoor sketching was never an activity that put great pressure on us. On a few occasions, Stan Roberts was able to borrow a Standard Vanguard from his older friend, Ted, thus giving us the luxury of being driven in style to the location that we had chosen for sketching - perhaps Rufford Old Hall. Needless to say, none of us had a car in those days, except for Brian Lewis who owned two Austin Sevens dating from the early 1930s, and that only rarely took to the road.

The time came when we decided to take the risk of having a morning off. It was one of those Easter heat waves and, inspired by the weather, we truthfully told Mr Howarth that we were going sketching on this occasion to Freshfield pine woods and beach. We boarded the electric train at Chapel Street Station armed, not just with sketchbooks and pencils, but also with swimming gear, towels and sunglasses, as well as flasks and sandwiches. There were about eight of us on the trip, anxious to find sheltered spots in the sand dunes for the soaking up of as much sunshine as we could. Everything was totally relaxed and soporific when, about an hour into our day, a tall figure in a long raincoat was spotted walking briskly with his rolled umbrella along the beach. It was Donald Howarth, dressed for a cold winter's day. Our initial amusement at his incongruous appearance was tempered by the frantic attempt to start producing sketches of the surrounding area in time to persuade him that we really were there to work. I don't think he was at all convinced, but he was such a nice man that he gave us the benefit of the doubt and waved us goodbye as he set off to return to Freshfield Station.

I am supposed to have announced, at the beginning of the session, that I would get a tan if it was the last thing I did. I was particularly foolish for, wearing only a pair of shorts, I lay in the sun from about ten o'clock in the morning until nearly six in the evening, by which time I resembled a lobster with a white band across the middle. Apart from the painful burning caused by over-exposure, I began to feel sick and, by the time I got home, it was clear that I was distinctly unwell. The doctor paid me a visit and referred me straight away to Southport Infirmary where I was admitted and stayed for three days, suffering from....sunstroke! Over that period, I was visited by several unsympathetic and highly amused fellow students, one of whom brought me a drawing of a bunch of grapes. I actually peeled twice, was unable to sleep for more than short periods and, for weeks, I could not lean back on a chair without extreme discomfort. The lesson was learned!

Only three months later I was working under the same sun near Peter Pan's Pool as a deck chair attendant during the summer vacation. It wasn't the worst job in the world, but the pay was meagre and, when the weather was bad, we were asked to put on waterproofs and to pick up litter from the beach, a quite disgusting way to earn a living. The main benefit for an 18-year-old was working with older men who were all quite adept at knocking the pretentious corners off students who thought they knew it all.

98

They were rough but kind, and the most entertaining of them was a little Belgian called 'Van' who continually made us laugh, despite our complete inability to understand a blind word he said, partly because of his accent, but also because he had a large pipe permanently in his mouth, a habit I had learned to avoid.

Although there was no prospect for me of renewing my acquaintance with Condor tobacco, I was tempted to try cigarettes. Unlike many schoolboys, I was never attracted to smoking as a younger teenager, but I was now developing the belief that a young man-about-town is more sophisticated with a cigarette in his hand. The timing was perfect, for there came onto the market a king-size filter cigarette called Peter Stuyvesant, ideal for beginners because it was so weak that you could hardly taste it. This was dangerous, for it enabled me to inhale without discomfort and, as we have all come to understand, inhaling is the first step to addiction. There followed another brand - Consulate, 'Cool as a mountain stream' - which conveyed the impression of being not only safe, but positively healthy, and its menthol flavour underlined the attraction. The problem, of course, was the cost, but several of the more popular brands, such as Capstan, Players, Senior Service, Woodbines and Park Drive, started selling packets of five, which were ideal for students. One or two of the smaller tobacconists would actually offer to sell you a single cigarette, and this gave me a commercial idea.

Southport Art School contained quite a lot of young smokers who were all short of money. What they needed, I deduced, was an on-campus facility to buy single cigarettes at a reasonable price. It was on this assumption that I started my cottage industry. I purchased Rizla cigarette papers, Golden Virginia rolling tobacco, a cigarette roller and a quantity of coloured gummed paper strips, designed for the making of Christmas paper chains. I produced a number of prototypes, which I smoked myself as part of a quality-control process. Within two days I had achieved what I considered to be a marketable product, but the finishing touch was the addition of the gummed paper strips, which gave some stability to the tip and, because they were coloured, endowed my cigarettes with an up-market status. Different tobaccos had tips of a particular colour to identify them, and the most expensive were gold.

'Baggy's Ciggies' enjoyed a promising start, although it must be said that the manufacturing process was exceedingly labour intensive. In a short time I built a clientele of regulars who purchased an average of three cigarettes each per day. The problem came as the business expanded, spread by word of mouth from satisfied clients. I simply could not keep up with the demand, and so I decided that, rather than stop trading, I would end the business in a triumphant gesture of sabotage. One of my most loyal customers was a boy called Robert, known to everyone as 'Scouse'. On the morning in question, I made a special cigarette for him from St Bruno pipe tobacco. It was a cruel thing to do, but at the time sadistic humour obscured the workings of conscience. Scouse paid his money and took his purchase, put it to his lips and struck a match. As he walked away from me I saw the habitual rise of his shoulders as he took his first long draught. This time his shoulders stayed up and he lifted onto his toes as he entered a prolonged asthmatic coughing fit. At the end, he turned his pale and anguished face towards me accusingly, muttering 'Bastard!' and disappeared down the length of the corridor. The word got round, and 'Baggy's Ciggies' declined as rapidly as they had risen, snuffed out by their creator.

GUILTY BY ASSOCIATION
Southport School of Art had a Students' Association whose purpose was to run social occasions for the student body. At the election early in the Autumn of 1956, completely to our surprise, Stan Roberts was elected chairman and I was elected secretary. It was something of a poisoned chalice for our predecessors had earned a rather dubious reputation for mismanaging the Association. Hardly anything had happened by way of organised socials, and it was rumoured that they had bought a motorbike out of official funds, although this was never established beyond doubt. In view of this, the Principal and staff were quite clearly pleased at our assuming of these posts of responsibility, hoping that social events would be run with more integrity than in the past. That would not be difficult.

Stan and I, supported by our friends, attacked our new assignment with great enthusiasm. We organised a Hallowe'en Hop within very short time and it was well supported, giving us an injection of funds, even though we broke all the safety rules in existence by having straw bales and candles burning in hollowed out turnips as part of our decorations. We insisted that, from now on, everyone join the Students' Association if they wanted to participate in whatever we arranged and, despite some grumbling about dictatorial methods, almost everybody paid their subscriptions. This symbolised support for our policies, but it also increased expectations, so it was important for us to deliver what we had promised.

The first major item in our calendar was the instituting of an Annual Fancy Dress Ball. The first one - "Nautical Nightmare" - took place in the Art School on Thursday, December 20th 1956 from 7.45 pm to 2 am. The music was provided by the Douglas de Belle Quartette and The Ark-Angels, and we laid on a cabaret that consisted of the satirising of our teachers and fellow students, and in which Barbara Barnett and I performed a sketch featuring Liberace. The tickets costing 8/6d were well-designed and printed in the college, and guests could choose between fancy and evening dress. It was a sell-out, and we were all greatly encouraged by the success. The problems came only after the event ended. Stan Roberts and I walked onto Hoghton Street to wait for the taxi we had called. Goodness knows how it happened (surely nothing to do with alcohol), but Stan suddenly realised that he was wearing only one of his patent leather shoes, and so the first job the taxi driver had was to drive slowly along the street whilst we scrutinised the gutter in the vain hope of spotting the missing footwear. We were just about to give up hope when it was found, but by half-past two in the morning Stan did not want to disturb his parents and so he came back to spend the night at our house, a plan that drew an icy comment from my mother.

The following year we were more ambitious, deciding to hold the event at the Palace Hotel, Birkdale, a huge place now demolished, apart from its pub, the Fishermen's Rest. The title of the ball was 'Oriental Fantasy', and we publicised it by making an enormous dragon, in which about twenty of us marched the length of Lord Street, rather in the style of a university rag parade. This, along with the interest shown by the Southport Visiter, guaranteed publicity, and this time Duggie de Belle's group was accompanied by Clarkson Woods and His Music. Our gamble of raising ticket prices to 12/6 also paid off, but anyone who bought after December 2nd paid 15/- and those who paid on the door had to stump up one guinea, a sure sign of our mounting confidence.

We continued to put on further dances, one of which was for a group of visiting students from Sweden. Their group leader, Per Lofquist, had approached our Principal, Harry Ratcliffe, to see if there could be some fraternisation with Art School students during their stay. We arranged a dance and buffet at the college, which did much to establish friendships with the Swedes in 1956 and for a number of years after that. Per's son, Stig, was a great character with very good English, and we did most of our arranging through him. On a different level, there was a blonde girl called Chastine who was by far the most beautiful creature I had ever set eyes on, and the story of my attempt to win her affection is told in the chapter after next.

In all modesty, we can claim to have left the Art School Students' Association in a much healthier state than the one we found when taking up office, and for several years into the future the momentum of this increased social activity and organisation persisted. One of the most heartening aspects was the number of former students who continued to attend the Arts Balls after they had left, and this included Stan and me. It was at an Arts Ball at the Palace Hotel in 1962 that I first heard the release of a song called 'Love Me Do' by a new group - The Beatles.

Southport School of Art

Footballers: Cyril, Dave, Colin, Eric, Brian, Myself, Mac and Rob

LOOKING BACK IN ANGER

The late Fifties was the period of 'Angry Young Men' - writers such as John Osborne (Look Back in Anger), Colin Wilson (The Outsider), John Braine (Room at the Top), Kingsley Amis (Lucky Jim), Alan Sillitoe (Saturday Night and Sunday Morning) and Keith Waterhouse (Billy Liar). Although they differed from each other, their common cause was the extent to which they all vigorously attacked the Establishment, just as Rock n' Roll did, but in a different way and for different reasons. One of the underlying motivations was that of class-consciousness, and this involved the need to undermine snobbery and to glorify ordinary, honest working people. Meanwhile, the novelist Nancy Mitford, an aristocrat herself, stirred the mixture provocatively by her writings about whether people's behaviour was 'U' (upper class) or 'non-U'. Greeting someone with "How do you do?" was U; saying "Pleased to meet you," was non-U.

For anyone who really wanted to be an angry young man, Southport at that time was the perfect target. It was snobbish, conservative, respectable, conformist, prosperous, 'refained', pretentious and easily shocked. It was a southern seaside oasis located in a Lancashire desert. Of course, I probably displayed a number of the characteristics I despised, but I had not yet reached a level of self-analysis enabling me to recognise my own hypocrisy. I searched avidly for something to be angry about but, because I was generally cheerful and optimistic, this proved quite difficult. I wasn't wealthy, but then the majority of people of our age were in a similar position, except for those Southport boys who drove large cars, courtesy of their rich daddies. I could be angry about that with some justification, but anger needs a stronger basis than envy. After all, if I had been lucky enough to have had a rich daddy, I should have done the same as they did. I could have been quite angry about those whose attitudes to life were conservative and resistant to change, except that I was also cautious when it came to the adopting of extreme ideas or the making of radical changes. When we all went to Harry's tailors in Princes Street to have our trousers tapered, I went for safe 17 inch bottoms, aiming to be in fashion, but not wishing to appear too extreme.

I was prepared to be moody, but not excessively so. I began to realise that I was not really cut out to be angry, and I was disappointed by my own failure to live up to the dissident's role, which was something I could justifiably blame on Southport. Why hadn't I been born and brought up in Wigan or Salford? This would have legitimised my discontent in a way that Southport never could. In the end, my scorn was directed against the safe target of those elderly ladies who came into the Art School in the

103

evenings for watercolour painting tuition. What did they know of art? How ridiculous were their cultivated upper-class accents, flavoured with Lancashire vowels! Fancy turning up for a painting class dressed for a cocktail party! This, then, was the object of my anger, although I must concede that it was not exactly the stuff of which the world's major social revolutions are made.

An event that added impetus to the search for social realism was the arrival on the staff of Harold Critchley. He was younger than the other staff and he brought with him a refreshing down-to-earth approach to painting. He resembled the boxer, Freddie Mills, and we were keen to win his approval. I made the worst of possible starts because, over the holidays, I had produced a large oil portrait of Beethoven. Even now I cringe at the very thought of it, and I excuse this ludicrous image on the grounds that it paid homage to my favourite composer. What Harold must have thought, when he first set eyes of this monstrosity, I cannot begin to imagine. Fortunately, I began to learn a little common sense under his influence, and I started a series of sombre blue paintings of interiors that, at least, had a small measure of artistic merit. The best of these featured an electric fire in an otherwise cold and bare room with a view down a dimly lit hallway in the background. Through the John Moores Exhibition at the Walker Gallery, Liverpool, we became conscious of social realist painters, such as Jack Smith and John Bratby who, like some of their literary contemporaries, glorified the mundane, and one of my later electric fire paintings, which measured 6 feet by 4 feet and cost an absolute fortune in oil paint, was very much a reflection of John Bratby's influence.

The change in society in the late 1950s was profound for young people and often threatening for their parents, who were hovering between maintaining authority over their teenage children, on the one hand, and displaying enlightened tolerance on the other. When I look back, I am convinced that many of the occasions when I defied my mother's wishes, I was driven by hormonal, rather than ideological, forces. The angst of the teenager can too easily be legitimised by sociological theory, but it was something almost all of us had to go through. If you are going to be angry, you might as well feel positive about it. Strangely, as the months went by, I quite forgot all about being angry at all.

Brian Lewis found a much more daring and exciting way of defying convention when, with Brian McCabe and Dave Berry, he swam across the Ribble estuary from north Southport to Lytham. In view of the treacherous tides and silt beds, this was a high-risk operation, but they had clearly done their research thoroughly and were roped together, swimming in a triangular formation. Brian Lewis's mother was distraught, and the Daily Express flew her in a light aircraft, in pursuit of her son and his comrades, following the report of a sighting from a shrimper to the coast guard. The plane arrived just in time to see those three adventurers starting their return journey, much to her horror. This was front page news the following day, and it put Brian well ahead of me in our quest to appear in newspapers as often as we could.

MAKING AN EXHIBITION

The jobs I had undertaken during summer vacations were not exactly career enhancing or prestigious - the biscuit warehouse, the stall at the fairground and the hiring out of deck chairs. Then, in July of 1957, I heard about Southport Corporation's plan to set up an open air art exhibition near to the bandstand in front of the Cambridge Hall. I applied to the Publicity and Attractions Department in the Cambridge Arcade and, to my great delight, was duly appointed. The pay of £7 per week was rather low, but the nature of the work was on a much higher plane than I had previously experienced. By far the most attractive aspect of the job was that I had become, within reasonable limitations, my own boss - I was the Curator of the Open Air Art Exhibition. Although I had occasional visits from David Lewis, my line manager, I was effectively autonomous, and my job carried greater status than any previous employment.

My duties consisted of moving the display screens on small wheels from a store in the Cambridge Hall - now the Arts Centre - onto the piazza in front of the Atkinson Art Gallery. Then, I collected the pictures, produced by a range of local amateur artists, and hung them on the screens. All I then had to do was sit with them throughout the day, negotiating any sales that were required and generally being charming to visitors. My friends could come and chat to me whenever they wanted, and I spent much of the time talking with visitors and friends whilst sitting in the sunshine. When it rained, I had the pleasant creative task of painting large murals on the interior walls of the Cambridge Hall. This not only displayed my work to the general public, but also resulted in my keeping, with permission of course, any of the oil paint and brushes that were left over at the end of the season, removing any need to spend on materials at least until Christmas. Apart from anything else, the painting of murals was considerably more fulfilling than my previous year's task of collecting litter on Southport beach in the rain.

The Swedish students were in town, and we were all at a party a few days before they were due to leave. During the evening, I spent some time with Chastine, the gorgeous creature I had first encountered at the Art School Dance we had organised to welcome them to Southport a few weeks before. I just had to invite Chastine to visit me at the Open Air Art Exhibition, and she agreed, much to my excitement. In describing Chastine,

Brian Lewis, Tradge and myself posing as artists in the painting studio

The author on duty as Curator of the Open Air Art Exhibition

I would compare her very much to a glamorous waif-like film star of the day, Mai Zetterling. This was just the perfect girl in the perfect setting.

That morning I spent twice as long as usual combing my hair, finding a clean shirt, and choosing a smart tie. I set up the exhibition and took my place at the table well ahead of the time she was due to arrive. I would give my Swedish guest a tour of the exhibition and then take her for lunch, whilst my friend, Brian Lewis, looked after the display. At 11 o'clock, I caught sight of a blonde head on the other side of the piazza. She was here! This was the ultimate achievement!

My delight was short-lived, for the blonde head belonged, not to the desirable Chastine, but to her close friend, Britmarie, whom I had met at the party along with the other Swedish students. I really do not wish to be unkind, but Britmarie was at least two stone heavier and four inches taller than I was, and my initial expectation of the arrival of a Scandinavian waif was now seriously unfulfilled. It was a bit like expecting Ulrika Johnson and getting Martin Johnson. "Chastine could not be coming, so I am come instead, in order that you may not perhaps be too greatly disappointed," explained Britmarie, beaming at me warmly. How kind, I thought, as my heart sank into my boots. I really could not believe the let-down. I was perhaps too greatly disappointed!

The following year I secured once again the curatorship of the Open Air Art Exhibition, and I was able to bolster my art materials by painting more murals. The Swedish party returned, but without Chastine on this occasion, so I had the pleasure of entertaining Stig Lofquist rather than his glamorous colleague. Nevertheless, it was the best vacation job I ever had and was certainly more relaxing than working behind a bar, which I chose to do for the summer holidays of the subsequent two years.

195819581958195819581958195819581958

A MATTER OF LIFE AND DEATH

From 1948 I had been a strong Manchester United supporter, and one of the best teams I can remember was that of the late 1950s. They drew Anderlecht of Belgium in the first round of the 1956 European Cup and won the away leg 2-0. Because the floodlights at Old Trafford were not yet ready for use, the home leg was played at Manchester City's ground. My cousin, John, and I were there, and I recall our amazement at the purple shirts that Anderlecht wore for the game. They might have looked good, but they didn't play too well, and United won 10-0. This was a talented young team built by Matt Busby, but no-one could have imagined the appalling drama that was to unfold eighteen months later.

United reached the semi-final of the European Cup, losing to Real

Madrid, then indisputably the best team in Europe, but they were in the competition the following year, defeating Shamrock Rovers and Dukla Prague before being drawn against Red Star Belgrade in the quarter-finals. They won the home leg 2-1 and went through by drawing 3-3 in Belgrade. The team set off for England via Germany, and the horror that struck United on the Munich runway is too well documented to require repeating.

The first I heard of the disaster was on my return home from Art School on the afternoon of February 6th 1958. As I wheeled my bike towards the side gate, my mother told me of the crash. I was completely stunned by the impact of this news, and I found myself incapable of thinking of anything else for the rest of the day. The following morning, I woke with a feeling of sickness, and only later was I able to connect the nausea with its cause as I read the morning paper, which gave a detailed report of the crash, the casualties and those fighting for their lives in hospital. I went into college wearing a black tie, bringing an incredulous comment from Harold Critchley, drawing my attention to the fact that I had not worn a black tie at the death of the Pope. Like me, Harold was a Catholic, and perhaps his remark was tongue-in-cheek, but it led me to conclude, at the time, that he had underestimated the scale of my devotion to Manchester United. The death of the Pope was most unfortunate. The destruction of part of my team at Munich was, to me at least, cataclysmic!

The team carried on its footballing commitments in league and cup, hastily signing new players to fill the gaps left by the casualties, as well as promoting youngsters like Bobby Charlton prematurely to senior roles. The tidal wave of emotion surrounding their efforts probably pushed them to achieve victories beyond their actual capabilities, and they reached the FA Cup Final against everyone's expectations, losing 2-0 to Bolton Wanderers. If anything confirmed my dedication to Manchester United, it was the air crash at Munich and the events of the succeeding three months. Of course, football is only a game, yet there are areas of human endeavour that overturn normal priorities. In a sense, Harold was right to question my black tie on February 7th, although he failed to distinguish what we should feel, as a matter of duty, from what we really *do* feel, if we are transparently honest. As Bill Shankly once remarked: "Football isn't a matter of life and death; it's much more important than that!".

SITTING WITH THE STRANGLERS

It seems most odd today to recount that I was twenty years old before I first visited the capital. Harry Ratcliffe, our Principal, was planning a journey to the Royal Academy with R.V. Pitchforth, one of the Academicians, and he thought it a good idea to take three students with him. So it was that Brian Lewis and Alan Kippax and I were chauffeured to London in the back of his Sunbeam Rapier. The highlight of our visit was on the first evening, which we spent at the Cy Laurie Jazz Club on the edge of Soho. Although Rock n' Roll was firmly established, Trad Jazz was still fine for both listening and dancing, and it had the added attraction of being seen as music for the more discerning. The Club was in a dark cellar with no ventilation and with condensation running down the walls as well as off the dancers. The music was extremely loud, but because it was live, the atmosphere generated was magnificent. In the midst of the activity, someone danced on his own with his hands in his pockets round and round a cylindrical red pillar in the room. His trance-like motion confirmed our suspicion that London was the place to experience the essence of youth culture. We decided that dancing alone was a slightly eccentric thing to do, and so we indulged in this new ritual, sporting our suits, ties and tapered trousers with seventeen-inch bottoms, courtesy of Harry's Tailors in Princes Street. This was life in the raw, and it was all a far cry from those silver-haired Southport ladies learning to paint in watercolour.

After a visit to the Royal Academy itself on the following morning, Brian, Alan and I headed for some of the more memorable sights. We walked down Whitehall, stopping to look at Downing Street, before entering Parliament Square. After exploring Westminster Abbey, we walked past the Houses of Parliament as far as the Victoria Tower, the arched doorway to which was open. Ordinary members of the public were entering, and so we decided to follow, although we did not know what lay ahead. As we reached the foot of a flight of stone stairs, I drew the attention of Brian and Alan to a notice, which read (or so I thought) "To the Stranglers' Gallery". Unaware of my mistake, and naively ignorant of quite what the building housed, we discussed excitedly the possibilities of what might lie at the top of the stairs. Although we had never heard of the Strangers' Gallery, we did recognise the House of Commons when we saw it, but I rather think that we were all just a little disappointed at the lack of drama in front of us. The Chamber of the House was hardly a substitute for the Chamber of Horrors!

TWENTY-ONE TODAY

Nowadays, eighteenth birthdays are seen as the beginning of adulthood. In 1958, twenty-one was perceived as the significant age of majority, and so that was the point at which the greatest fuss was made. My own twenty-first party was highly enjoyable, and the present of a Grundig reel-to-reel tape recorder, for which my mother must have made quite considerable sacrifices to afford, was the last word in luxury for me at that time. My first recording was of the Top Twenty off David Jacob's radio programme, and the hit records at that time included 'Stupid Cupid' by Connie Francis, 'Hoot's Mon' by Lord Rockingham's XI, and 'It's only make believe' by a singer with the amazing name of Conway Twitty. The quality of reproduction seemed wonderful, yet it was still only mono in those days. Despite this, my own anniversary has been overshadowed in my memory by the unforgettable events at a similar celebration, four months earlier, of my friend Stan Roberts' twenty-first birthday.

Stan had arranged to hold his party at Alty's Lane in Ormskirk at the house of his girlfriend, Carol Hutchinson. The house was large and had a superb hi-fi system designed by Carol's father, so it was the ideal party setting. Those of us from Southport hired a minibus to take us to Ormskirk, and this was my first date with a new girlfriend, Barbara, whom I had met at previous parties. Stan came round to ask us all what we would like to drink. I replied that I would leave it to my host to mix me something special and so, with no inkling of what lay ahead, I agreed. He returned with a very large brandy glass, at least half-filled with a brown liquid, which I sipped and smiled my approval. I wasn't aware of its contents, but that did not seem to matter. Only much later was I told that the cocktail contained equal parts of gin, vodka, dry Martini and sweet Martini. Unaware of the implications, I cheerfully ordered a refill some time later and, between eight o'clock and half-past midnight, I drank with enthusiasm no less than five of these dangerous potions from a bubble glass holding at least half a pint of liquid.

Although I had been aware of not following the conversation for some time, it was only when I rose from my chair to go to the loo, fell onto all fours, and discovered that I couldn't get up, that the extent of my incapacity became apparent. Three friends half carried me upstairs to the bathroom, where I vomited with a violence previously not experienced. I was laid onto a single bed in a room occupied by another groaning alcohol victim, Alan Kippax. There was 'contemporary' wallpaper in the bedroom with large brightly-coloured geometric shapes, and I could not bear to look at it. However, when I closed my eyes, the sensation of floating was even worse, and so I was trapped in an intolerable state of other-worldliness.

Meanwhile, poor Barbara, whom I had neglected for most of the party, was being looked after by Brian Lewis - always willing to help a damsel in distress. I was wakened at two in the morning to be told that the minibus had arrived and would leave for Southport in five minutes. With considerable help, I made the journey from bedroom to the pavement and was lifted into the vehicle. I went to sleep, waking as we entered Scarisbrick New Road just before King George V School. Thinking it was time to get off, I stood up, slid back the side door of the minibus, and began to step out onto the pavement. As the vehicle was travelling at over fifty miles an hour, I was saved by the prompt intervention of other party-goers.

When the vehicle arrived at my door, I was carried semi-conscious up to bed where I slept for a further fifteen hours. Just like the sunstroke of two years before, I had to go to the edge of the precipice in order to learn the value of moderation. I was ill for three days with alcohol poisoning, unable to concentrate on anything, incapable of focusing my eyes, vomiting frequently despite an aversion to eating, paralysed with diarrhoea, and racked with a permanent sick headache. I have to admit that I was to be drunk on a number of subsequent occasions in my formative years, one of which was an evening when Philip McLean and I recklessly drank copious bottles of Worthington White Shield and walked home, making sand pies along the middle of Weld Road, Birkdale, at one o'clock in the morning with a bucket and spade we had found in a garden. However, there was never to be a repeat of the extreme over-indulgence I had committed at Stan Roberts' twenty-first. May God (and Barbara) forgive me.

1959195919591959195919591959195919591959

PUTTING ON THE STYLE

No matter how short of money we are, there are times when it is worth splashing out just for the hell of it. A perfect example of 'mutton dressed as lamb' occurred one sunny morning when Eric Appleton, Donald Holt and I went sketching at Southport Pier. In those days there were landaus parked on the Promenade, and these most elegant horse-drawn carriages were available for hire to anyone who could afford the price. By half-past ten, we had completed all the sketching we needed and were just about to walk back to college when an idea came to us. We emptied our pockets and discovered that, between us, we could just afford to return by landau instead of on foot. We travelled at gentle trotting pace, practising our 'Queen Mother' waves, down Nevill Street, Lord Street, Hill Street and across Hoghton Street. As our carriage reached Mornington Road, we beamed with pleasure at the prospect of arriving in royal style at the front of the School of Art to the envy of our friends as they returned from morning break at the refectory. Almost inevitably, our arrival was just about two minutes later than planned, and our expensive and flamboyant display remained completely unwitnessed.

Riding in a landau is clearly not a serious attempt to impress. Sitting in the Basket Lounge of the Bold Hotel, wearing a blazer and tie, whilst sipping whisky and dry ginger and smoking a black and gold Sobranie Black Russian cigarette, represents a more meaningful expression of decadent opulence. On the two occasions when I worked behind a bar during the summer holidays, this was how I spent one hour of my day off, indulging in the most contrasting behaviour I could conceive to the mundane occupation of barman. It was a very 'Southport' thing to do, particularly in those days, but the motives underpinning it are probably no different from the reasons why people buy lottery tickets today. The ambience was the diametric opposite of the working-class social realism I had so wanted to embrace only two years before, which shows how transitory one's ideological outlook can be at that age.

Southport has always been well off for clubs, and in 1959 there was a wide choice of alternative drinking venues. We thought that supping in one of these was a more sophisticated way to spend our evenings than in an ordinary pub, and so we decided to join the Carstairs Club, situated down a narrow entry on Lord Street between what is now the BT shop and the HSBC Bank. It was small, with room for no more than about twenty-five people, and was run by Bruce Carstairs, who very much resembled a character from British movies of the 1950s played by someone like George Sanders, and who spoke to us in the manner of a wartime RAF officer. Brian Lewis and I went to the Carstairs club about twice a week, accompanied by a new friend, Colin Graham, whom Brian had known before. However, the Club was transformed to a more down-to-earth atmosphere when, a few years later, it was bought by Norman Ashurst, father of one of my Trans X form-mates from KGV.

Another popular venue was the Glen Park Club, which was located down a flight of stairs in a long basement under Boothroyd's on Lord Street. It was much larger than the Carstairs club, and was owned and run by Tony Costello and Barry Ward, two young entrepreneurs who managed to attract a celebrated clientele, including Peter Alliss, the golfer. Brian Lewis often did stints behind the bar, and I also helped out on odd occasions. Because the club was regularly open until one or two o'clock in the morning, not a common occurrence in those days, Tony would add a taxi fare to the staff pay, and I recall him once handing an envelope to Brian Lewis and saying, "Here's your taxi money, Brian. Now get on your bike and bugger off!" Tony was a magnetic and enterprising personality who seemed much more grown-up, confident and streetwise than us, even though he was hardly older than we were. Barry Ward, on the other hand, was in his early thirties and more retiring in manner, but we guessed that he was the one who put up most of the money. I remember being shocked a few years later to hear that Barry had died of a heart attack, a sobering prospect indeed for all of us.

Our lifestyles were slowly improving, but one of the major steps forward was in transport. For most of the time, my own travelling was on bike or bus or foot, apart from occasional trips in the Standard Vanguard that Stan borrowed from his friend, Ted, or the jaunts in one of Donald Holt's many bangers. A new student, Rosemary Wright, had arrived at the

Art School, and she soon became close friends with Stan, Carol and myself. Rosemary was extravert and amusing, but one of her greatest assets was the ability to borrow her mother's Vauxhall Cresta more or less at will. We could now travel to parties in an enormous pink and white automobile, which resembled a cross between a double bed and a wedding cake, but sumptuous in its comfort. This was the stuff of which dreams really are made. Who wants John Osborne's 'Look Back in Anger' when you can have John Braine's 'Room at the Top'?

THE OTHER SIDE OF THE BAR

I had been thoroughly spoiled as Curator of the Open Air Art Exhibition, my vacation job for the previous two summers. For some reason, the corporation decided against holding the event for a third time, so I was forced to look elsewhere for holiday employment. Working behind a bar seemed a good idea, for I had enjoyed the occasional stint at the Glen Park, where there was seldom any work pressure. I applied for, and was appointed to, the job of barman at the Crown Inn on Coronation Walk, managed by Frank Howe who was something of a formidable figure, but a kindly man nonetheless. In my ignorance, I had made the assumption that all I had to do was stand behind the bar and serve drinks, not having considered the other tasks of carrying in crates of bottles, stacking shelves, wiping tables, cleaning ashtrays, sweeping floors, collecting litter, washing glasses, checking optics, and so on. After finishing my first session at half-past two, I cycled home, lay on the settee and slept for over an hour. Being an artist and struggling with visual concepts may be tough, but it is no substitute for real work, as I was about to discover.

The second day was much, much worse. It was Orange Day, the annual invasion of Southport by thousands of Liverpool people who were intent on parading, singing, eating, drinking and generally getting their money's-worth from this special occasion. The pub was heaving with revellers, all wanting serving immediately. In general, they had brought food with them, and some of the women had half bottles of gin and rum in their handbags. Frank told us to refuse no-one, even if we thought they had already had too much to drink and, with the agreement of the Police, we didn't close for the mid afternoon break, on the basis that getting people out of the pub would cause more trouble than it was worth. The staff went for lunch in shifts to a café two doors down the road. This was, indeed, a baptism of fire for me, but it was good experience in terms of acquiring life skills.

As time went by I became accustomed to the work demands at the Crown Inn, and I also adjusted to the rough and tumble of everyday life in a pub. I have no doubt at all that occupations such as these for naive younger people like me were invaluable as induction processes into adulthood. Although you can quite easily form the belief that you know it all at twenty years of age, it takes a dose of real employment to inform you just how sheltered and narrow your life has been. Initially, I was most put off by some of the Pleasureland stall holders who came to the bar and shouted, "Ey, lad! Give us a pint!" Although I still find rudeness off-putting, I have learned not to be upset by it, particularly if it is a reflection of culture rather than of malice. I have found, too, that many people who exhibit a gruff exterior have a deep reservoir of kindness and compassion within them, masked by the embarrassment of showing emotion.

There was another difficulty I faced during my time behind the bar, but this was a physical one. A number of people in their late teens or early twenties suffered from strange post-adolescent complaints, and mine was nose bleeds. Although I had experienced the problem for a few years, it became intense in the summer of 1959. The only way I could handle it, whilst discharging my duties, was to pack one of my nostrils with cotton wool. This did not always work for, if the bleeding was intense, the blood would take an alternative route down the other nostril. In desperation, I packed the second one, and my appearance at the bar under these circumstances must have been hideous. One of the actions that exacerbated the bleeding came at the end of the evening session. Frank allowed us all a staff drink when the towels went on the pumps, and my choice in those days was a bottle of Worthington White Shield. I imagine that this strong sediment bitter had a higher volatility than most beers for, within ten seconds of taking my first mouthful, blood would pour out of my nose at high speed.

This had been the summer of Cliff Richard's 'Living Doll', and also of a more or less disastrous camping trip to Tal-y-llyn near Dolgelly, that Eric, Tradge, Don and I took before the end of the holidays. We all had a little money to spend from our vacation jobs, but our general organisation was chaotic, our tent erecting was slipshod, and our cooking techniques were basic in the extreme, culminating in our ground sheet being covered in boiling hot beans and tomato sauce as the primus stove collapsed under weight of a pan far too big for it. We spent much of our time at a nearby pub learning advanced snooker shots from a Welshman called Hamish. Although I had not realised it, this was my final dose of irresponsibility before embarking on teacher training a few weeks later. As my computer sometimes asks: "Are you sure you want to do this?".

AS ONE DOOR CLOSES

As our National Diploma course was drawing to a close, we began to paint at a dramatically increased rate, mainly because we all needed to

The author with Tradge, Eric and Don's car in Dolgelly

'Interior with Electric Fire' - 6ft by 4ft - 1959 - P D Bagshaw

submit folios of work - in my case painting and lithography - that reflected two years of dedicated study. When, in January 1959, I laid out the fruits of my achievement over that period, my stomach sank at both the quantity and quality of what I had to offer, and it was then that I started two major pieces of work. One was an abstract impressionist painting in blue (inevitably) that turned out to be the best work I ever produced before or since. It consisted of landscape-type shapes with layers of transparent glazes superimposed on them, and the style was a mixture of Peter Lanyon and John Piper. Unfortunately, I took no photographic record of it before I gave it to Valerie Hinton, one of my friends on the ATD Course at Liverpool. The other was a very large picture entitled 'Interior with electric fire', following on from previous works, but on a much grander scale and painted, rather in the style of Bratby, in thick impasto colours of olive green, orange and yellow. These two pictures probably saved me from a disastrous result, and the last-minute-panic approach to the completing of assignments is one with which many young male students will be readily able to identify.

Leaving Southport School of Art was not a wrench for me. I had been more than happy there, but I was ready for the next stage - my final year of being a student. Armed with my new qualification of National Diploma in Design, I began studying for the Art Teachers' Diploma at the Liverpool Regional College of Art in September, 1959. I was quite fortunate to have gained a place on the course, for no-one at Southport had advised me about application dates and so, once it was discovered that I had missed the deadline, the Principal had to plead with Liverpool to allow me to be interviewed after the course had already been filled. This they did, and I was pleased to find that my interview performance persuaded them to create an extra place for me. I travelled from Southport by train on that first morning and walked from Exchange Station to the College on the corner of Hope Street and Mount Street to join the sixty other members of the course.

The head of the ATD course was Alan Tankard, a man with the build of the comedian, Fred Emney, and the voice of Liverpool's own Derek Guyler. He wore a long grey mackintosh and a trilby hat, even when he addressed us in the lecture theatre. "I started this course, y'know. Oh yes, I started it," he informed us all on several occasions in that first term. He was assisted by a strange assortment of colleagues. Sylvia H was a slender and fragile woman with a cut-glass accent, and her responsibility was to teach us the History and Philosophy of Education. She was doubtless a good academic, but the content of her lectures was light-years away from the grim realities of the teaching practice we were soon to encounter. Although Plato and Socrates were clearly worthy of further study, neither

116

made any mention, as far as I could discover, of recommended methods of issuing art equipment to forty-seven nine-year-olds in an Edge Lane Primary School.

John Hart had his feet more firmly on the ground, which was fortunate because he had to instruct us in the Curriculum and Practice of Education, but there still seemed to exist in his lectures and seminars a gulf between theory and practical reality. It was almost as though no-one wanted to commit themselves to addressing the mundane, everyday problems we wanted to raise, and they justified this avoidance by telling us that we would all have to find our own answers in our own way. True as this may have been in a long-term context, it felt to us very much like an easy way out for them at the time.

By far the most delightfully eccentric tutor was George Meyer-Marten who lectured in Aesthetics. He was aged about sixty and was a small man with long silver hair, giving him the appearance of a nineteenth century composer. I think the person he most resembled was a shorter version of the first 'Dr Who', as played by William Hartnell. His Austro-Hungarian accent, very much like that of the scientist Heinz Wolf of 'Great Egg Race' fame, was fascinating, imparting a mellifluously elegant style to quite ordinary words. I found myself listening to the sound, rather than to the meaning, of his lectures, which was not helping me at all. His slowly-enunciated sentences were labyrinthine, groaning under the weight of dependant clauses. A typical example of this might be: "If you vish to consider, or ozerwise contemplate, ze merits, and of coze ze de-merits insofar as zey may or may not exist, of a given set of phenomena, zen you will inevitably be confronted - I say 'inevitably, realising that nossing is strictly inevitable - viz a set of criteria relating, to a greater or lesser extent, or perhaps not even relating at ole, to whatever may be ze objects of your investigative processes." We would nod sagely, understanding very little of what he was driving at, but immensely impressed by the apparent scholarship of it all.

There were several stories circulating then in the department about George Meyer-Marten's achievements, and I have no reason to doubt their truth. One was that he had swum for Hungary in the 1936 Olympic Games held in Berlin; the other that he was the first man to drop a bomb, for test purposes, in Europe. These were so exotic that we believed them unreservedly. A talent we did know about was that he was an accomplished, if rather flamboyant, violinist who played regularly in a string quartet in Liverpool. My new friend, John Mockett, once had a conversation with the great man about his wish to attend one of his recitals, but thought he had better point out that he might be a little late because he had to travel back to the recital from West Derby where he was

117

on teaching practice on that afternoon. Meyer-Marten welcomed his interest and said, "By ole means come late if you hev to, but please make sure zat, when you enter ze room, you step in time to ze music".

John Mockett was also intrigued by George Meyer-Marten's and, for that matter Alan Tankard's, refusal to admit to mistakes or ignorance. GMM was once lecturing to us about onomatopoeia in language and was pointing out that words beginning with 'str' were always rapid and abrupt, giving examples such a 'strike' and 'strip' and 'strafe'. "What about 'stroll'?" asked John. "Ah.. well... stroll.. er.. originally.. er.. meant.. 'to walk quickly" replied GMM, clearly fibbing to save his face. On another occasion we were writing notes at the end of a seminar, and John, who had invented his own personal shorthand, which incidentally was later published, was using it to take a record of the discussion. Alan Tankard, leaning over his shoulder, and still wearing the long mac and the trilby, said, "Ah, shorthand. I can read that, y'know. Oh yes, I can read that." This was plainly untrue, but John's obtuse sense of humour prompted him to hand in an essay to Alan Tankard written entirely in his own shorthand. When it came back, it had been marked with comments in the margin such as 'a good point' and 'this is well-argued'. "The old fraud," observed John with a smile, yet it must be said that we had a genuine fondness and admiration for our course leader.

For students, Liverpool was a much grander stage than Southport could ever be. Everything seemed larger, louder, riskier and more pulsating. Fashions were more extreme, the arts were more prominent and accessible, and we were only a stone's throw from the Anglican Cathedral and the Philharmonic Hall. This was the year of the launch of the Mini and the Ford Anglia, and the explosion of Liverpool music was only two years away. Pubs, too, were more exciting, particularly our local, Ye Cracke, where we went regularly for a lunchtime pint and cheese roll. To this day, it is the most crowded pub I have ever entered, and how we ever got to the bar to make our order is a miracle. Everyone was so crushed together that, if you put your hand in your pocket for money, you had great difficulty getting it out again. If we could afford it we would have the occasional lunch at the Bluebird on Renshaw Street, but usually we walked down Leece Street to have a three-course business lunch for the absolute bargain price of two shillings and threepence (about 12p) at the Tai Ping Restaurant on the corner. When it rained, only the back of the restaurant was available because the roof leaked, requiring them to cordon off the front section. When we paid, it was to an elderly Chinese with a long beard who calculated our costs on an ancient bead frame. One of our favourite sweets was Honolulu Pudding, which consisted of fluorescent yellow sponge covered in fluorescent pink custard.

Socially, Liverpool was varied and exciting, and there seemed to be parties going on everywhere. One I went to was at the house of Adrian Henri, the artist and poet who was then beginning to emerge as a leading cultural figure in the city. His home was in Faulkner Square, a decaying environment which had clearly been a most prosperous residential area in an earlier time, but which now had become a haunt of prostitutes and other shady characters. On the corner was the Portuguese Consulate, announcing its identity with a tattered national flag. The party was enjoyable, if a little pretentious. We were all provided with bowls of soup and bread rolls, whilst people sat cross-legged on the floor reading aloud their poetry to the accompaniment of modern jazz. It would have seemed innovatory had not the Sitwells' conducted similar activities in the 1930s.

Meanwhile, the party scene in Southport seemed to be looking up at that time. During the Autumn of 1959, Colin Graham and I, with a few other friends, went to huge all-night parties at a big house in Trafalgar Road, Birkdale, which was once raided by the Police, not in relation to drugs or anything like that, but because some of the neighbours had complained about excessive noise at three o'clock in the morning. They did have a point, for there must have been over three hundred of us on the four floors of the house, not just from Southport, but also from as far afield as Preston, Wigan and Liverpool. Colin and I produced satirical radio-type programmes on my Grundig tape recorder for playing at the parties. They were continuations of experiments I had conducted with my cousin John a year or two earlier, and they consisted of a series of quick-fire sketches, interviews and spoof investigative reports about serious and not-so-serious subjects, occasionally satirising some of the better-known Southport personalities. The programmes were called 'Dirge for the Proud World', a title borrowed from one of my father's books of War Poems, and the theme tune was an extract from Beethoven's Choral Symphony, now used as the European Anthem. The humour was a mixture of the Goon Show, Beachcomber, and 'Just Fancy', interspersed with sound effects such as machine guns, flushing lavatories and explosions, and they went down wonderfully well at these parties, often drawing prolonged applause and cheering from the drunken listeners.

By half-term, we had all settled in happily at Liverpool, excited at making new friends and undergoing new experiences. Despite the girls on our course outnumbering the boys by more than three to one, we soon formed a football team with the help of some Liverpool NDD students, and I arranged a fixture against my old friends from Southport School of Art, which we unfortunately lost. The other item of interest I recall is that both John Lennon and Stuart Sutcliffe were students at the College of Art at the same time as I was. After the Quarrymen era, the group was renamed as 'Johnny and the Moondogs', but changed to 'The Silver Beetles' in the early part of 1960, but I cannot claim that they were friends of mine.

So, I had arrived in Liverpool. All I now had to do was to prove that I could teach.

PRACTISING THE ART

Many students on postgraduate teaching courses undertake school practice on a block basis. On our ATD course, teaching practice ran throughout the entire three terms for one and a half days per week. This was both better, insofar as it gave us time to recover between the sessions, and worse because it denied us a realistic insight into the considerable difficulty of sustaining an energy-sapping work routine for five consecutive days. We were unlikely to complain, for it was a system ideal for beginners. My own practice consisted of Tuesdays at Stanley Secondary Modern School in Marshside, Southport, and Wednesday afternoons at Northway County Primary School near Edge Lane in Wavertree, Liverpool. After Christmas I would be spending the entire one and a half days at Merchant Taylors' School, an independent boys' school in Crosby.

The purpose of the first week was to observe lessons and to meet the head and staff of the school we would be operating in for the academic year. Northway was a busy, happy, slightly frantic school catering for children from an area of the city which was far from prosperous. The first shock I had was the size of the classes I would soon be teaching; forty-five in one and forty-seven in the other. They were taught by two male teachers, Mr Tharm and Mr Collins. They were pleasant and helpful to me, but I formed the clear impression that they were both delighted and relieved at the prospect of my taking over their classes on Wednesday afternoons. I observed Mr Tharm's lesson on that first visit. The children were generally well behaved, if rather noisy, and I noticed that, about every thirty seconds, Mr Tharm would say 'sshhh!' to the class. They took no notice, and I suspect that he didn't realise he was doing it, so ingrained this habit appeared to be.

The following week, my first two lessons at Northway went reasonably well. The children listened politely to me and, despite their excitement at the novelty of a different teacher, they were well behaved, mainly because I managed to keep them occupied throughout both sessions. Mr Tharm and Mr Collins each made a very brief appearance at the commencement of the lessons with their own groups, and then left, telling me to come to the staff room if I required any assistance. My main problem was in giving the children the attention that they needed and required. It was my aim to speak to everyone in the room at least once - a principle I attempted to maintain throughout my career - but within classes of over 50 in size, this was far from easy. The only odd feature of that first encounter was the behaviour of a boy named Colin, who disregarded entirely what I had asked the class to do, and sat at his desk carefully drawing figures, each having heads in the shape of a television picture. Since he caused no trouble, I decided to leave him to it, but I did have doubts about how his time was spent at home. At the end of the lesson he put up his hand. "Yes, Colin." *"Please sir, me drawring's all gozzy!"*

I caught the bus back to the centre of Liverpool with a feeling of satisfaction. Although I had not set the world of education alight, my lessons had gone as planned, the children seemed to like me, and I had not needed help of any kind from the two members of staff. As the train moved out of Exchange Station on the way to Southport I began to feel drowsy, partly because of sun coming through the window into the crowded railway carriage, but largely as a result of having expended much physical and emotional energy in teaching my first lessons. As the train stopped with a jerk on entering Seaforth & Litherland, I awoke with my head in the newspaper of the businessman opposite. I smiled and apologised, but he ignored me. At Waterloo, there was a repeat performance, and also a third and fourth at Blundellsands and Hightown where, fortunately, he got off. I don't know why I was surprised by my fatigue, but I was. I suppose I thought that the most tiring experiences were physical ones, like working behind a bar, but I was just beginning to realise how easy my life had been thus far. I was about to find out, for the very first time, the real meaning of hard work.

The Head of Art at Stanley Secondary Modern School was Jack Warburton, and he could not have been more welcoming to me. Jack treated me like a colleague, as did many of the staff, including the Head of Physical Education, Ken Houldcroft. A former KGV boy and member of Spencer's house was on practice at Stanley at the same time, but he did not endear himself to staff by his announcement that he was a graduate, mistakenly assuming that none of those who teach in secondary moderns have degrees. On my observation day, Jack announced to the class of fourteen-year-olds that they were lucky to have me teach them because I was considered the best art teacher in the north-west of England. Even for Jack, this was a bit over the top, but it did nothing to harm my self-confidence, which can be amazingly fragile during a year such as this one. Children are experienced at being pupils, whilst my own supreme self-assurance as a student was beginning to evaporate as I learned how exposed and vulnerable young teachers can be.

The term at Stanley was wonderful, teaching me what it meant to feel a true part of the school community. Because the staff and children were so friendly, I became involved in more than art teaching, and one more unusual activity I performed was in an end of term cabaret where I played the part of Fred in the Avon's hit song 'Seven Little Girls Sitting in the Back Seat'. I was somewhat embarrassed because one of the staff, who was first choice for the part, was asked by the Fourth Year girls to stand down so that I could play the rôle. He took it very well, but it was part of a problem, if a nice one, that I encountered whenever I taught this Fourth Year group. About six of the girls had red hair and, as they lined up at the door at the end of the lesson, some of them wanted to kiss me goodbye and say "See you next week!" as they left. Well, I suppose someone had to do it!

The most disastrous lesson of that period was one I had planned carefully for Mr Tharm's class at Northway. We had free access at the College to whatever materials were required for teaching practice, and so I helped myself to quantities of balsa wood, strong cotton, expensive coloured tissue paper and forty-seven pairs of scissors to take into the lesson. The plan was to make mobiles of large fish that the children would design using balsa wood as the frame with tissue stretched over it, rather like model aircraft used to be made. They would then bring their fish out to me so that I, standing on a table in the middle of the room, could hang them from a structure of balsa strips suspended on cotton threads from a ceiling beam. The idea was to produce a moving sculpture that resembled an aquarium - an exciting project, or so I thought.

The mistake that destroyed my kinetic dream was forgetting to bring glue with me, and I was forced to borrow from Mr Tharm's cupboard. Unfortunately, the only glue I could find was that horrible sticky stuff that looks like toffee and smells of fish. In the absence of an alternative, it would simply have to do. I had laid out all the equipment on the desks before the children returned from their break, and I gave them a brief instruction on what they had to do. They set about their task with great enthusiasm, but worked much more quickly than I had anticipated. This is one of the great dilemmas for student teachers who find out about the difficulty of occupying children when your lesson plan has left you with half an hour to spare. Luckily, that did not happen on this occasion.

"Right, everybody, now bring out your fish to me as soon as they are ready," I announced from my position on the table where I was struggling to construct the network of balsa struts as quickly as I could. The first fish arrived from a boy named Anthony, who was under pressure to work faster than the other children because he had to leave early to attend his choir rehearsal at Liverpool Cathedral. "How nice, Anthony," I remarked as I took from him an object resembling a folded turquoise umbrella dripping with toffee glue. This was followed by similar sticky creations, all suffering from the fact that the glue was heavier than the tissue. Already recognising that my plan had failed completely, but not wishing to disappoint the class, I hung a succession of glutinous, dripping objects onto the structure which, quite inevitably, broke under the weight as it grew in size. Then, a wonderful thing happened. The bell rang.

I surveyed the room, full of happy children, delighting in the products of their efforts, with glue in their hair, on their pullovers, on the scissors, on the desks, on the chairs and on the floor. "Right, stop work everybody." *"Can we stay and finish our fish?"* "NO!!.. er, no, Philip, I'm afraid there isn't time for that." *"We'll help you clear up, then."* "Listen, just leave everything as it is and go!" *"OK, see yer next week, sir / Tara, sir / Bye, sir / Sir, how do I get glue out of me hair, sir?"* The room emptied, and I spent forty tedious minutes clearing up the chaos and restoring the room to some sort of normality. I travelled home in despair, stinking of fish glue, on a crowded bus and an icy-cold train that broke down twice and, when I got home, my front door key broke off in the lock. "Now remember,you can learn just as much from a failure, everyone, as you can from a success," Sylvia H once informed us. Bollocks!

196019601960196019601960196019601960

CATCHING THE DISEASE

I simply could not wait for the new term to start in January, 1960, such was my enthusiasm for teaching. John Mockett and I just lived for Tuesdays and Wednesdays when we could get to grips with classroom practice, rather than endure the relatively dull theoretical aspects of the course at college. By contrast, most of our colleagues were relieved when Thursdays came and they could escape from the anxieties of teaching to the safety of lectures and seminars, a view we simply could not understand. I was now absolutely certain that I had chosen the right career, and I was quite anxious to accumulate as much experience as possible before I started as a fully-fledged member of the profession.

John Mockett was a strong influence on me at that time, and also for at least ten years afterwards. He was a dour, intelligent Lancashire boy, living in Adlington, near Chorley. As well as artistic achievements, he had a talent for languages, in particular for French which he later taught, and he was also a most accomplished church organist. In addition, he was a brilliant mimic, and our shared sense of humour led us into a series of very silly, but very funny, practical jokes on quite a regular basis. That our careers were somewhat parallel gave the two of us much to discuss in the way of comparing experiences, and it was a considerable pleasure to find a kindred spirit who viewed the job of teaching just as seriously, and enjoyed it every bit as much, as I did myself.

Merchant Taylors' School

Stanley Secondary Modern School

My teaching practice would now be at Merchant Taylors' for the remainder of the academic year. Although I had enjoyed and learned from my time at Northway, my preference was for secondary, rather than for primary, teaching. In addition, Crosby was a much easier journey than Wavertree from Birkdale, and this used up less travelling time and, most important to a student, less expense in travel costs. Merchant Taylors' School could not possibly have been a greater contrast to Northway County Primary. I reported to reception, and a message was sent to the head of the art department, Trevor Hughes. Before he arrived, I was ushered into the study of Mr Yorke, the Headmaster, who welcomed me to the school and expressed the hope that my teaching practice would be a fruitful experience. He was friendly in manner, but I felt rather like a convicted defendant appearing before a judge for sentencing. Trevor Hughes introduced himself and took me to the staff room for a cup of coffee before the beginning of morning school. I quickly learned that members of staff each had their own chairs, and that I must be most careful not to sit in them. Through the window I could see the school's Combined Cadet Force parading in the quadrangle, with senior boys screaming orders to those in the ranks. It made me feel even more uneasy than I was already, and I suddenly wished myself back in Wavertree.

Compared with Jack Warburton at Stanley, Trevor himself was rather cold and formal, but when I observed him teaching in the same style, I realised that his distant manner was nothing to do with his view of me, but was simply a reflection of his personality. The art department was highly organised with everything in its correct place and, although I initially found this rather off-putting, I later came to appreciate the advantages of operating a highly efficient system. I started my teaching programme in the second week, and I must say that the boys worked peacefully and efficiently at everything I asked them to do. Despite this, there was very little in the way of enthusiasm. When a boy put up his hand, it was to ask if he might leave his place to get another brush, rather than to ask an artistic question about the work I had set. The only exception was a Lower Fifth class which contained a number of extravert personalities, and I found this group much more stimulating and pleasant to teach than the rest. Trevor was quite helpful in his appraisal of my performance, but I soon discovered that praise was a rare commodity and that I would have to earn it the hard way.

My second inspection visit was upon me, and I was desperately keen to produce an effective lesson, not so much to impress my tutor, John Hart, but mainly to squeeze a few words of praise from Trevor Hughes. Even before the lesson began there was a small drama. John Hart arrived only five minutes before the start, dressed in an immaculate grey suit and white shirt, but with his hands covered in engine oil as a result of car trouble on the way to the school. This confusion seemed to help by taking the conversation off myself, and I went on to give the very best lesson I had taught at any of the three schools up to that date. John was very complimentary, but left early to continue the struggle with his vehicle. Trevor then said to me "I thought, on the whole, your lesson went reasonably well." I was aghast. By his standards this was fulsome praise indeed, and it taught me that prizes are more precious when they are hard won. I was now ready to teach.

THE END OF FREEDOM

Seductive as the student life may be, there inevitably comes a time when it is outgrown, and I had arrived at that point in my development. I imagine that it marked the last chapter of youth and the first of adulthood, the passage from boy to man. My friends Brian Lewis and Philip McLean had chosen to do their National Service first, and spent two years in the RAF. I contemplated the prospect of my own two-year stint in the forces with a heavy heart, for I was burning to start my teaching career at the earliest possible date. Then, God moved in a mysterious way, and National Service was ended in the early part of 1960. We were free, and all of us now faced the task of securing employment for the coming September. John Mockett and I decided we would apply only to Grammar Schools, a plan which one of my former tutors at Southport School of Art told me was a waste of time. Nevertheless, our optimism was rewarded, and I was appointed to the Blessed John Rigby Grammar School at Orrell, near Wigan, whilst John secured a similar post at Cardinal Allen Grammar School in West Derby, Liverpool. Not long after that, we learned that we had been awarded the ATD, meaning that we would be paid as graduates in our new posts.

I was so excited by the thought of my forthcoming job that I bought a car. It was a 1937 Vauxhall Fourteen with six cylinders and a serious oil leak, and Donald Holt sold it to me for £30. It was big and black, with an arm rest in the back, and it would not have looked out of place in 1930s Chicago. Unfortunately, I had not yet passed my driving test, and so I was restricted to night-time runs down the Formby by-pass with headlights that didn't work and with my foot flat on the floor to coax 70 mph out of the huge engine. I polished it, admired it, sat in it and painted white walls on the tyres to give it the style of a limousine. On one occasion, at great risk, I took five of my friends for a run, and the engine stalled on the level crossing at Birkdale Station, with the car just clearing the gates. In those days there was a Town Hall, a Library and a Police Station at Birkdale, and the two traffic policemen in a patrol car laughed as my five friends pushed the heavy car so that I could get it started. It was the closest shave I ever had, because my offences, had I been charged, would have been 'driving without a licence', 'driving whilst uninsured' and 'driving without working headlights'.

In summer, I did one more stint behind the bar at the Crown Inn, but my heart was not in it and I found myself becoming increasingly annoyed by the behaviour of some of the drinkers. We used to get coach parties of silver-haired women arriving from Blackburn, Chorley and other Lancashire towns, and they would fill the pub with screams of laughter about every thirty seconds. All they were doing was enjoying themselves, but I found this so irritating that, on one occasion when I was slicing a lemon for a gin and tonic, I threw half of the fruit at the noisiest group. It hit the wall about six inches above a woman's head, stuck there for a moment, and then slid down the wall out of sight. None of the women at the table was aware of my action, which was just as well, for I should have deserved sacking on the spot. However, this symbolised my unsuitability for continuing, and I resigned the next day after only four of my planned six weeks. Clearly, it was time to undertake something more fulfilling.

Freedom is both an ending and a beginning. I was free from being a student, yet the constraints of working as a teacher freed me to operate in a new and strangely seductive environment. This was the end of boyhood, which is a long period stretching from birth to the point where you have to consider the needs of someone other than yourself, and manhood, which started for me when work started. I was anxious to enter that world.

POSTSCRIPT

I remember quite clearly reckoning in 1960 that, by the beginning of the year 2000, I would be 62. As my father had died at 57, I wondered whether I would live beyond that age. I also assumed that I would be a different person from the one of twenty-two years of age. I had not understood that what we are is, effectively, a product of what we have been. The child is the father of the man, just as Wordsworth asserted. As for some of those who shared my boyhood, I list their own achievements:

John Howells, my cousin, gained a BSc in Dairy Technology at Reading University, managed a Stilton Dairy, lectured at Reaseheath Agricultural College, and has worked for the EU as an expert in Russia, Kyrgyzstan, Turkmenistan and Montenegro. When in this country, he lives with his wife Jennifer in the village of Thursley, near Godalming.

Philip McLean gained a French degree from Keble College, Oxford. He worked for the Reed Paper Group and Shultons before entering the Foreign Office, where he had postings in Bolivia, Washington, Algeria, Boston, Beijing, where he was the Deputy Ambassador. He completed his career as Her Majesty's Ambassador in Havana. He married Dorothy Kirkby and they live in Goring-on-Thames.

Brian Lewis joined me in teaching at the John Rigby Grammar School, Orrell, where he later became Head of the Art Department and then Senior Teacher at its change to a Sixth Form College. I was Best Man at the wedding of Brian and his wife, Carol, who live in Southport.

Stan Roberts married former fellow-student from Southport Art School, Carol Hutchinson, and became Divisional General Manager of the Agricultural Division of Allied Colloids. They live in Westhead.

John Mockett became Deputy Head and, later, Headteacher at Campion School, St Helens before moving to St.Augustine's. To my great sorrow, he died at the age of fifty-seven in 1994. His widow Sheila teaches French at a Manchester high school.

Harold Critchley, my tutor at Art School, was appointed Principal of St Helens College of Art, and lived in Rainford with his wife, Joan. I am godfather to youngest son, Paul. Sadly, Harold died in April 2001.

Geoffrey Dixon, my headmaster at King George V School, is still an active member of the Old Georgians' Association, and was elected Chairman in 2000-1, marking the 75th Anniversary of the opening of King George V School. He lives in Southport with his wife, Nancy.

My brother Denis became Radar Installation Inspector for the MoD. He and his wife Jay celebrated their Golden Wedding in 1999.

Susan, my niece and godchild, married Dan Murphy and they live in the Warwickshire countryside. Their son Ben has just completed Officer Training at the Royal Military Academy, Sandhurst, and daughter Claire is reading a Sports & Leisure degree at Chichester. I am so proud of them.

My mother died in 1988 just after reaching her 90th birthday, with all her faculties and still doing the Telegraph crossword. I have so much to thank her for, not least for supporting me through higher education.

*

'The Diary of a Southport Boy' is no more than a recall of past experiences, none of which was recorded at the time. Memory functions are complicated, and I have been surprised by how far the remembering of one episode can lead unexpectedly to the recall of another. One day, perhaps, I will attempt to continue this project with 'The Diary of a Southport Man'. If I do, it will tell of amusing, touching. fulfilling and depressing experiences in twenty-nine years of teaching, of receiving the surprise gift of a car, of the inside of a psychiatric ward, of a Master's Degree year in Cardiff, and of the highs and lows of running a video production company.

Most of us think we have one book within us, but the difficulties lie in transforming ideas into action and in making time to write the thing. Whether or not I have the resolve for a second remains to be seen.